Praise for Janet Bloch's Workshops and Seminars on Marketing for Visual Artists

• • • • •

"I worked with Janet at a critical juncture in my career, where I was re-entering the art/gallery world after a long hiatus. She provided a critical eye for my work, editorial guidance for my statement and résumé, and many leads for exhibition and grant opportunities. Her advice and support at that time was instrumental in giving me confidence to pursue these opportunities; she gave me the tools and the motivation to go forward."

— *Kate Friedman, mixed media artist*

• • • • •

"I am now more selective when entering certain shows. I no longer feel the pressure to 'Enter Now!' to a show that isn't reflective of the images that I am trying to project with my art. I feel comfortable taking the time to research. I feel more confident in presenting my work in written language."

— *John Gray, painter*

• • • • •

"Janet gave me the direction, motivation, and confidence to get my work out in public. And the path she sent me on has taken me to venues I never dreamed of, and leadership skills I never knew I had!"

— *Sandra Holubow, painter*

• • • • •

“Janet has helped me with many career questions, but most significant has been her synthesis of my disparate artist statements into one. After using it for over two years, I find it still expresses my core ideas and has been easy to adjust for specific applications.”

— *Corinne D. Peterson, sculptor*

• • • • •

“Janet Bloch’s advice was invaluable to me in taking my career to a new level. I now have the knowledge and resources I need to confidently approach new exhibiting prospects in a professional manner. New doors are opening for me all over the place.”

— *Shari Pettis, painter*

• • • • •

“Janet has spoken at our conference for many years. Now, all of this vital information is gathered together into one workbook that any artist can utilize to help them reach their desired success. This is a “must” for any emerging artist who wants to make a career in the arts.”

— *Amy Rogers, Director, Self-Employment in the Arts Conference*

• • • • •

“Janet’s guidance and advice was invaluable to my ability to execute the artist’s marketing process. She knows what to do, how to do it and when to do it. Her broad experience and knowledgeable guidance offers a comprehensive and clear direction that I could find nowhere else.”

— *Susie Smith Trees, sculptor*

Strategic Marketing Tools for Visual Artists

Janet Bloch

published by

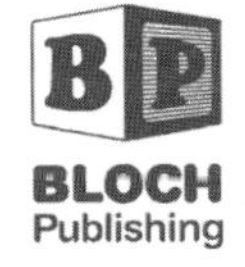

Chesterton, Indiana

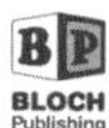

Strategic Marketing Tools for Visual Artists

Published by
Bloch Publishing
497 Highland Drive
Chesterton, Indiana 46304

Cover Painting
© 2010 Janet Bloch, *Power Wise,* acrylic and latex on panel, 48" x 36"

Book and Cover Design by Jeanie James, Shorebird Media

ISBN 978-0-615-41857-5
Library of Congress Control Number: 2010919049

Trade paperback
10 9 8 7 6 5 4 3 2 1

Printed in the United States of America

Table of Contents

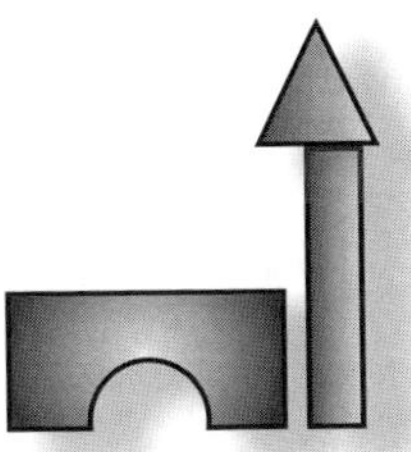

Introduction

In 1980 I received a Master of Fine Arts degree from the School of the Art Institute of Chicago. When I left school, I had absolutely no idea how to get my artwork exhibited. Like many art students, I had one question: ***What next?***

Happily, I can report that many art schools now realize the importance of providing career-building information to students. However, there is still a serious lack of information for students regarding strategies for embarking on a successful art career. And, of course, there is the problem of imparting these strategies to artists who are not and have never been art-school students.

I decided to write this workbook to reach as many artists as possible who hunger for this information, as I did. There is a great deal of mystery about the art world and its workings. As a result, artists often feel like outsiders. Combining this common perception with the competitive and secretive world of art can fuel the artist's sense of isolation and insecurity. Fortunately, I'm in a unique position to help.

As an artist, I share a mindset with many of the artists I've met. I've felt alternately insecure and grandiose, often within an hour's time. I've believed wholeheartedly in my work while dreading rejection. I've been frustrated by a lack of knowledge about the gallery system but longed to be a part of it.

A great shift in my perspective occurred when I directed Woman Made Gallery in Chicago from 1993 to 2000. Woman Made is a nonprofit gallery whose goal is to support women in the arts by providing opportunities, awareness, and advocacy. During my work there, I came to understand the "other side" of the art business—the nonartist side. I learned what makes a great submission packet, what belongs in an artist's statement, and what steps should be taken to build an impressive résumé. It became clear to me why gallery owners are protective of their time, why they want materials presented in specific ways, and what they consider unprofessional behavior. I learned from other artists' successes and failures.

As a result of learning this information, I've received numerous grants, including an Illinois Arts Council Fellowship, an NEA Regional Visual Artists Fellowship, and two Indiana Arts Commission Grants. My work has been represented by prominent Chicago galleries since 1996, and I've also had many solo and two-person exhibition opportunities in nonprofit institutions. Recently, I made it to the finalist phase of two premier public art projects. These successes are the direct outcome of employing all the information I learned from other artists.

Most of this knowledge I gained experientially and bit by bit. Over the following pages, I wish to impart my experience so that you don't have to wait years to piece together all this information. You don't have to reinvent the wheel! My desire to educate artists stems from a spiritual axiom that I was introduced to years ago. The saying is this: What you desire most for yourself, give to others. When I was starting out, I always wished that I had a mentor, someone "in the know" who could advise me about what to do and what to avoid. Now that I've gained that knowledge through my experiences, I wish to share it with others. I can say with all sincerity that I hope you will synthesize this knowledge and go on to succeed beyond your wildest dreams.

Let's begin!

Chapter 1 *Get Out Your Maps*

The Big Vision

When I work with clients one-on-one or in workshops, my first request is that they tell me what their ultimate vision is for their art career. I ask the same of you. Your vision need not be set in stone, especially at the beginning of your career. I am interested in the kind of art career you envision for yourself from where you are now.

Formulating and stating your dream enables you to begin your journey on the road to success. Like any traveler, you must know your starting point and your desired destination.

Later in this chapter we will determine your starting point, but for now, I want to get you excited about your future. In order to do this, you have to allow yourself to dream and not get bogged down with self-doubt.

Destination

Before you state your goal, please consider different aspects of the art world. For example, an artist who is solely interested in making money will take a different route than will an artist whose objective is to be a critical success. While the two objectives are not mutually exclusive, the truth is that many artists who participate in outdoor fairs and craft shows may make much more money than artists who exhibit in small museums. But it is unlikely that even artists who have won many awards at outdoor fairs will receive a review by an art critic in a newspaper or magazine. So you can see that it is essential for you spend some time thinking about the kind of career you hope to have.

Defining success

An artist with a successful critical career is defined as an artist who has garnered tangible praise in the form of awards, exhibitions, and reviews by professionals in the art world. Respected professionals in the field include museum curators, art critics, and well-known artists. The more prestigious the museum or art journal the curator or writer is associated with, the more the artist's credentials are validated.

An artist with a successful critical career is defined as an artist who has garnered tangible praise in the form of awards, exhibitions, and reviews by professionals in the art world. Respected professionals in the field include museum curators, art critics, and well-known artists. The more prestigious the museum or art journal the curator or writer is associated with, the more the artist's credentials are validated.

I advise you to be expansive in your career vision. Go ahead and dream BIG! I'll help you set realistic goals along the way, but I think it's important to inspire yourself first. Here are some sample goals to illustrate what I mean by dreaming big.

My Big Vision is to:

- Be sought after for public art commissions.
- Earn a good living painting pet portraits for famous people.
- Have my art represented in museum collections across the United States.
- Make $100,000 a year painting *ketubahs* (Jewish marriage licenses).
- Create one-of-a-kind works in glass for heads of state and corporations.

Assignment: *Use this space to write your Big Vision for your career.*

Starting Point

Getting you in touch with your Big Vision is designed to point you in the right direction toward your goal. Now let's examine where you stand in relation to this goal.

Please answer the following questions as honestly as you can:

- ☐ Have you completed a body of work?
- ☐ Have you exhibited your work in group shows? If yes, where?
- ☐ Have you exhibited your work in a solo show before? If so, where?
- ☐ Do you know what your work is about?
- ☐ Do you have an artist's statement?
- ☐ Do you have an artist's résumé?
- ☐ Have you sold your work before? How much did you sell your work for?
- ☐ Have you received commissions?
- ☐ Has your work won awards?
- ☐ Have you received any grants or been accepted to any artist's residencies? (See Chapter 11 for more information on grants and residencies.)
- ☐ Are there any professionals in your field who champion your work?

Body of Work

A body of work is defined as a group of 10 to 20 pieces of art, depending on their size or scope, that are related by medium and content. If you're a student, it's likely that you have some paintings, sculptures, and drawings that you're proud of and have done for classes. However, this is not a body of work. A body of work explores the same themes and usually is in the same medium—for example, all oil paint, all collage, all bronze. The works can easily be identified as being by the same artist. It may take an artist a year or more to develop a body of work. You might think of a solo show in a gallery as the result of a body of work.

Now review your answers and begin to assess what actions you need to take to get to your goals. Do you need a lot more time to create artwork? Do you need to develop your artist's statement? Do you need to explore exhibition opportunities in order to build your résumé?

You've now begun to take a good look at where you are at this moment. Having completed this exercise, you may be feeling overwhelmed. Please don't be discouraged by your findings, as I can assure you that you can move your career forward no matter where you stand on the road to success. It does take hard work and patience, and there is no magic formula, but my purpose in writing this workbook is to give you very detailed information about what materials you need and how to proceed.

A Word About This Journey

Using the traveler analogy once more, let's suppose that you want to travel by car from Florida to California. There are several ways to approach the trip. You can drive sixteen hours a day, whizzing past natural wonders, museums, and restaurants. You can sleep in your car and eat fast food. Or you can meander, stopping every twenty miles to talk, eat, and take a stroll at each gas station, rest stop, and street corner—and perhaps never arrive in California at all.

Another approach is to pace yourself on this journey, stopping in select cities and small towns of interest along the way. You can choose to take in cultural sights and sounds, eat at wonderful restaurants, and learn new things about people and places.

It is my hope that you will approach your journey in the last way, and that the smaller goals you set toward your Big Vision will be an enjoyable and vital part of your experience. Respect yourself and this process so that you don't reduce your life's passion to a mad dash for the finish line. However, I also caution you not to get sidetracked by trivialities so that you lose sight of where you're going.

In Chapter 12 of this book, we'll create a strategic plan. In the next chapters, I'll arm you with the information you need to follow the plan. This is your journey, but I'll be accompanying you as your guide. I hope to make the logistics of your trip easier.

Chapter Notes

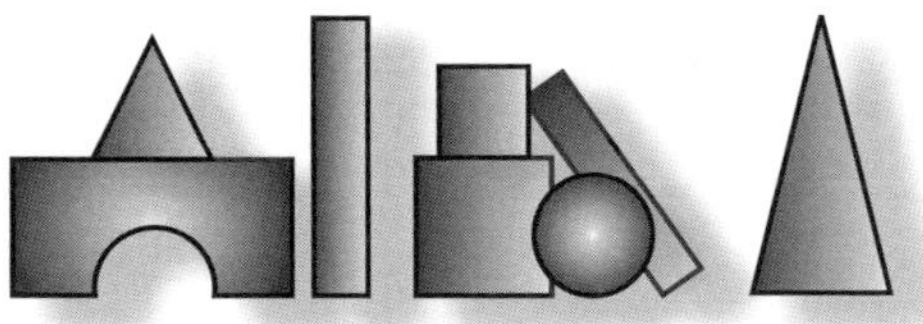

Chapter 2 *The Packet*

A packet is the basic submission proposal for artists who are applying for grants, residencies, solo shows, public art projects, and gallery representation. The purpose of your packet is to wow the target viewer(s) so that you're selected for the sought-after opportunity. Just as you would pack necessary items, such as a toothbrush and underwear, for a trip, you must compile the essentials in your artist packet. The components are almost always the same. These are:

- Visuals
- Image list
- Résumé
- Statement
- Cover letter or proposal

If you are just beginning your career, it is likely you will need to build up the components listed above before you send out a packet for a solo show or gallery representation. In order to build your exhibition history, you will want to enter and be accepted into many group shows and competitions before you submit packets for solo show opportunities. The essentials for entering group competitions are much fewer than the ones required for a packet. You wouldn't need to pack as many things for a weekend jaunt as you would if you were going traveling for a month.

For a juried competition you will most likely be

asked to send digital images of three artworks. One important factor in entering a group competition is to make sure all three images are consistent in content and media. I address the best strategies for images in the following chapter. Most group show entries do not ask for a résumé, and if you send any unrequested items, they will probably be tossed out. An entry fee is a standard requirement for entering work in juried shows. I've seen entry fees range from $15 to $40, with an average request of $25. I wouldn't enter too many shows that cost more than $25 at the beginning stage of your career.

The items I have listed for the packet may vary in their exact details from one venue's guidelines to another, but the basic categories are the same. In Chapters 3–9 we'll go over each of them in detail.

The excellence of each of the elements in your packet is the key to persuading a gallery director to take further interest in your work—or a panel of jurors to select you for an artist's residency. Simply having average-to-good materials won't be enough to give you a competitive edge in the art business. There are more good artists than there are opportunities for them, so you need to put together the best packet possible if you're serious about succeeding.

If you're missing one or more of the items listed, or if after reading this book, you conclude that your elements fail to meet the highest standards, then you'll need to address these weak spots. I advise you to create or revise these components as part of your six-month action plan. (See Chapter 12.)

Before crafting a packet you should always go to the website of the place you want to send it. Look to see if they have specific guidelines posted. For instance, a gallery's website may state a particular time of year when they review packets. If that time of year is June and July, it's best not to send your packet in August, as it will sit there for almost a year before it's reviewed. There's a good chance your packet will get misplaced in that amount of time. In this case, the best time to send the packet is in April or May. That way the packet will contain your most recent work and get to the venue in plenty of time. The website might also indicate if the gallery is participating in an important exposition such as Art Chicago or Art Basel. Sending a packet right before or after the gallery is engaged in this type of event isn't a great idea because the staff is busier than usual. I'd also avoid sending a packet out in the period from Thanksgiving through New Year's Day, unless there's a deadline for a submission request during that time.

A gallery or other venue may also post the exact items they want you to send. Send only the items they request. Most likely, anything you send that is not requested will be thrown out. People have given thought to the guidelines, so please respect them. If they ask for ten jpegs (a jpeg is a type of digital file) on a CD, do not send twelve. If they specify that the images should be formatted to a specific size, you must learn how to resize your digital images or pay someone to do this for you.

Once you put together the elements of an outstanding packet, tweaking the particulars to suit different guidelines will not be as time-consuming as it is in the beginning. More important, you will see a definite increase in the number of positive responses you receive for your efforts.

Assignment: *Go to the websites of several different galleries and art centers. Look for the submission guidelines for each venue. Print them out and compare and contrast them. Note whether some spaces request different materials than others do. Use the table on the next page to note the materials you need and the dates to submit for each venue. A sample is filled out for you.*

Name of Venue (Sample) Center for the Arts 1234 Renoir Place Rome, Georgia 54321-0000				Phone: Fax: Contact: Contact e-mail:	800-555-1212 567-555-1212 Andre White AWhite@lcarts.org	
# of Images	Image List	Resume	Statement	Letter or Proposal	Other Materials	When to Send
10 - 20	✓	✓	✓	✓	Reviews, catalogs	January and May

Name of Venue				Phone: Fax: Contact: Contact e-mail:		
# of Images	Image List	Resume	Statement	Letter or Proposal	Other Materials	When to Send

Name of Venue				Phone: Fax: Contact: Contact e-mail:		
# of Images	Image List	Resume	Statement	Letter or Proposal	Other Materials	When to Send

Name of Venue				Phone: Fax: Contact: Contact e-mail:		
# of Images	Image List	Resume	Statement	Letter or Proposal	Other Materials	When to Send

Name of Venue	Phone: Fax: Contact: Contact e-mail:	

# of Images	Image List	Resume	Statement	Letter or Proposal	Other Materials	When to Send

Name of Venue	Phone: Fax: Contact: Contact e-mail:	

# of Images	Image List	Resume	Statement	Letter or Proposal	Other Materials	When to Send

Name of Venue	Phone: Fax: Contact: Contact e-mail:	

# of Images	Image List	Resume	Statement	Letter or Proposal	Other Materials	When to Send

Name of Venue	Phone: Fax: Contact: Contact e-mail:	

# of Images	Image List	Resume	Statement	Letter or Proposal	Other Materials	When to Send

Chapter Notes

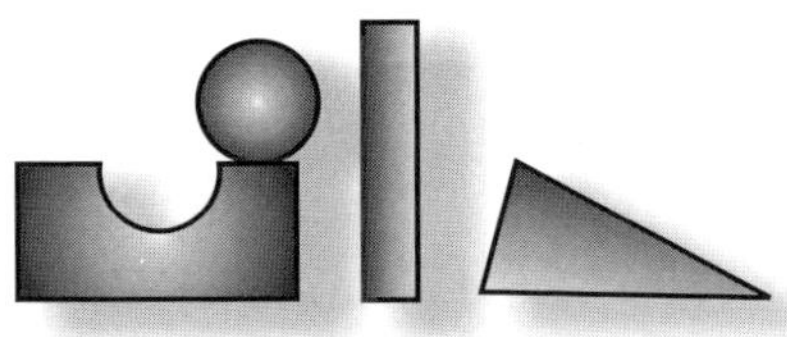

Chapter 3 *Visuals*

What Is a Visual?

A visual is a photographic representation of your work. Visuals are by far the most important part of your packet. You need visuals that are impeccable to succeed in the art world. Each photographic image should represent your artwork accurately and to its best advantage. It shouldn't look better than the actual work, but it can emphasize the dramatic effect of the work. For example, if the work is sculptural, you will want an image of the most interesting angle of the piece with the lighting arranged so that shadows cast by the piece give the work more force.

Artists are now expected to submit digital images for review to most grants and exhibitions. Admittedly, formatting digital images in the myriad of size requirements that may be requested is more time-consuming for artists than labeling slides. I also realize that many artists are confused about how to do this, because the process depends on the software one uses. However, I don't wish to debate this issue here.

The bottom line: You must learn how to use the appropriate software (such as PhotoShop) or get someone who knows how to help you. Otherwise, you will miss out on most of the important opportunities in the art world.

Slides vs. Digital Images

At the time of this writing, slides are no longer the customary way to submit images of your artwork for opportunities. The digital image, formatted as a jpeg and burned onto a compact disk, attached to an e-mail, or uploaded to an Internet site, is now the accepted standard. If you already have slides, there are companies that do an excellent job of converting them to digital images. One company I recommend can be found at *iprintfromhome.com.* However, you still need to know how to resize your scans for the variety of demanded requirements.

How Do I Get Visuals?

Some artists manage to do a very good job of taking their own images, though most that I have seen do not. However, many photographers are not adept at taking photographs of artwork. I can't tell you how many times I've seen very poor images of artwork that an artist paid someone to take. The only way you can evaluate whether you or a photographer has done a good job is to scrutinize your images for their accuracy against the real artwork.

When looking for a photographer, insist on seeing images of other artists' works that he or she has shot. Someone who takes beautiful photographs of landscapes or people may not be any good at taking photographs of artwork. It requires different equipment and different skills. Artists who live in a small town may have to travel to a larger city to get their work documented. Or, if there is a museum in your area, you can call the institution and see if they can refer you to the photographer who photographs their collection.

What Makes a Good Visual?

If you aren't sure whether you have good visuals, here is a checklist of elements to help you evaluate your images.

☐ **There are no distracting elements in the image**.

This means no light switches, fingers, or floor moldings. No trees or grass unless the work is an outdoor installation. Your couch, carpet, or cat should not appear in the photograph. Such elements are not a part of your artwork and serve only to convey the message that you are inexperienced or don't care about the presentation of your work. Fabric (especially wrinkled fabric), corrugated cardboard, and other makeshift backgrounds are not suitable backdrops for artwork.

☐ **The color is correct.**

Color differences between the actual artwork and the photographic image should be imperceptible. You should not have to explain to anyone that the color is really much more vibrant in person—or more subtle or less harsh.

Please see the color plates on pages 55-58

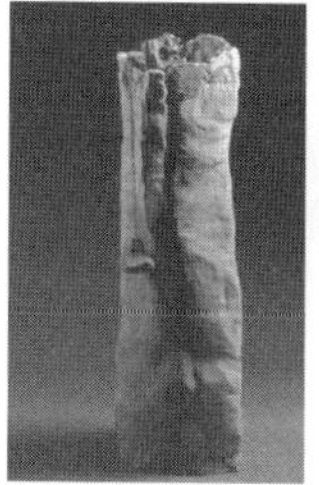
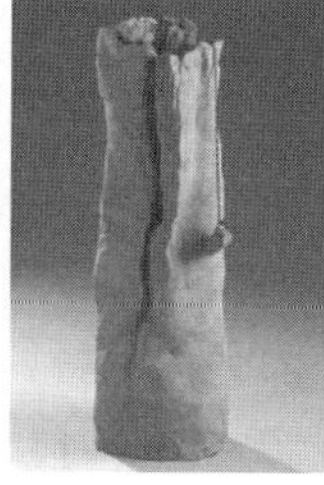

Color Illustration 1 – p.55

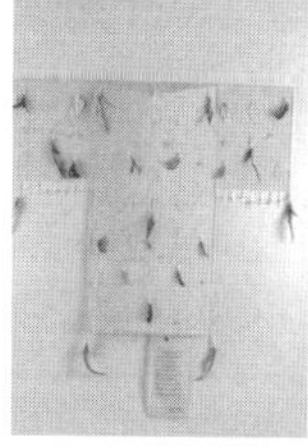
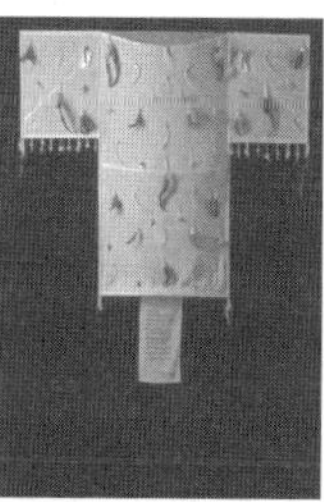

Color Illustration 2 – p.56

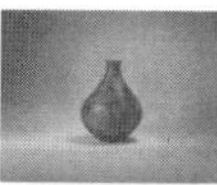
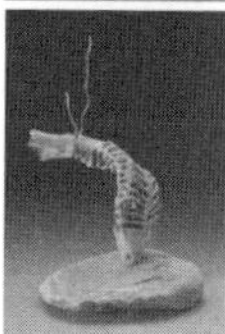

Color Illustration 3 – p.57

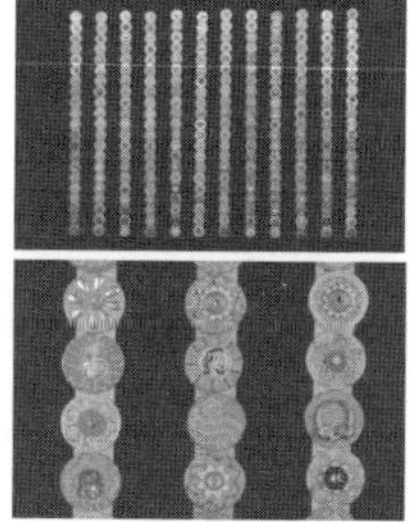

Color Illustration 4 – p.58

☐ **The artwork is large enough in the photographic frame.**

☐ **The lighting is correct.** [See Illustration 1.]

This means not too dark, not washed out, no "hot spots." If there are shadows for three-dimensional work, they should be intentional and placed where you want them. This requires working with a photographer who can adjust the lighting for this purpose without compromising the image quality of the artwork. Two-dimensional work should not cast shadows.

☐ **The background color choice enhances the artwork**. [See Illustration 2.]

One of the pluses of digital images (as opposed to slides) is that you can crop all the background from two-dimensional work on your computer. Backdrop papers that have a sweep of color from black to gray are nice for three-dimensional work. I advise against using fabric as a background.

☐ **The photograph is in focus.** [See Illustration 3.]

Of course, you will not knowingly send blurry images out for a proposal. But it takes a discerning eye to distinguish a sharp image from one that is of a lesser quality. My photographer uses a medium-format digital camera, and this makes a big difference in the image quality.

If your work is 36 inches x 36 inches or smaller, there's absolutely no reason for any part of your image to be hard to make out. If it is, get a new photographer.

☐ **The image shows enough detail.** [See Illustration 4.]

If a work is very large and/or made up of a lot of detailed materials or components (such as an artist's book with many pages), you will want to have several detail images photographed and choose the best one.

Details A detail is a close-up image of your artwork that imparts more information about your materials and/or technique. Examples:

- For a large textile work, a detail shows intricate stitching.
- In a large painting, a detail shows the brushwork.
- For a sculpture or an installation made up of various materials, a detail reveals the types of media used and/or the way each is used.

A detail image might also present an alternate view. Examples:

- For an artist's book, a detail could show an impressive or representative page.
- For three-dimensional works that are very different from one side to another, details could show various perspectives.

I recommend that you do not overuse detail shots. You do not need more than one detail per artwork unless the work is room-size and you are submitting it for an entire show. For two-dimensional work, I wouldn't include more than two details in a packet of ten works. Always put the shot of the whole piece first and then directly follow it with the detail. Put the artworks with details near the beginning of your visuals so they give the viewer the information they need to be able to comprehend the rest of your work.

Some juried shows won't accept detail shots. You'll need to decide how integral a detail is in understanding your work in order to decide if these shows make sense for you to enter.

The images tell a story. Order the images in your packet so they flow and tell a story. Don't start out with the most complicated images. Allow the viewer to ease into an understanding of your work and let the complexity build. You also want to put the images in a sequence that reads logically. For example, if there is a progression of sizes, don't put the smallest work adjacent to the largest piece, but instead let the sizes build.

While maintaining logic and readability, you also want to keep your audience engaged. When the progression gets too predictable or the art pieces are very similar, the viewer will get complacent. You need to spice up the sequence just enough to get the viewer's full attention.

The images are consistent.

When you send a packet, whether it consists of three, ten, or twenty images, your artwork and vision should remain consistent. Don't send a variety of types of work in the hope that the viewer will like one of them. This rarely proves successful. I've sat with numerous jurors, and I've never met an arts professional who selected an artist for an exhibition based on versatility. Jurors are interested in those who have developed their vision. They aren't interested in seeing one drawing, one painting, and one sculpture—or one landscape, one portrait, and one abstract work. This communicates that the artist is still a student and has not developed a unique artistic voice.

Send the correct number of images.

A standard application for many juried group exhibitions allows you to send up to three artworks. Always send the maximum number of works allowed. If the exhibition allows you to submit three images, do not send one or two. This constitutes a weak entry and leaves the juror wondering if you're simply not productive.

A word of caution: Some group competitions allow you to submit three works for one fee and then allow you to add more images for an additional fee. My opinion is if a juror doesn't like your first three images, he or she won't like your next three, so save your money. If you aren't able to convince the juror with the three images permitted for the basic fee, then move on.

This rule applies only when sending images to group shows. The guidelines for a solo exhibit or a public art opportunity usually request 10 to 20 images. In this case, my suggestion is to send 14 to 18 images. My reasoning for this is that a packet of 20 does not feel as though it has been edited. A submission of 14 to 18 consistent, strong works communicates a body of work large enough to translate into a solo show, yet also conveys that you have refined your selections.

Assignment: *Look at the photographic images of your artwork with a new critical eye. Make a list of elements that could be improved upon referencing the list given in this chapter. If you do not have photographs of your own artwork yet, then go to several websites of various artists and critique the quality of their images, evaluating them against the criteria given.*

Chapter Notes

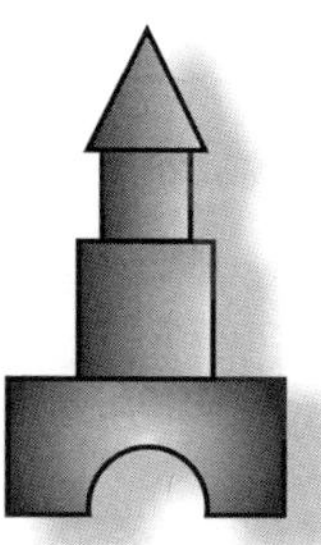

Chapter 4 *Image List*

An image list is a document that corresponds to the images you're sending out in whatever form they take: prints or digital images on a CD. The purpose of an image list is to provide more information about the images you are sending in a clear and orderly manner.

The minimum information that the list usually contains is:

- Your contact information
- Title of the artwork
- Year the work was created
- Media used to create the work
- Dimensions of the work

You may also be asked to provide:

- Prices
- An explanation of each piece
- A thumbnail image of each piece. (A thumbnail is a very small image of the artwork.)

Formatting Your Image List

One of my favorite ways to organize an image list is to create a table. (See sample, page 22.) I realize that everyone isn't equally computer literate, but I urge you all to learn to use the Table menu if you use Microsoft Word. However, if you don't know how to use it and don't foresee learning anytime soon, just type a standard list. Either way, please make sure of the following:

Your digital image files are numbered appropriately.

If you're given specific directives for labeling your digital image files, please follow the instructions to the letter. If specifics aren't given, make sure that your files correspond to your image list. I wish I had a nickel for all the images I receive from artists that have nothing to do with the accompanying list. It wastes my time. If you send out your materials this way, you will appear unprofessional. Check your list against the order of your images before you send out your packet.

Most of the confusion happens when sending digital images on disks. The jpeg images need to be titled with a number prior to the title of the work. Otherwise, the computer will burn your images on the disk in alphabetical order of the artwork's titles. This is problematic if this is not the order in which you want the images to be viewed. Furthermore, if you have more than nine images on the disk, you must start the numbering with *01.Title*, then *02.Title, 03.Title,* and so forth.

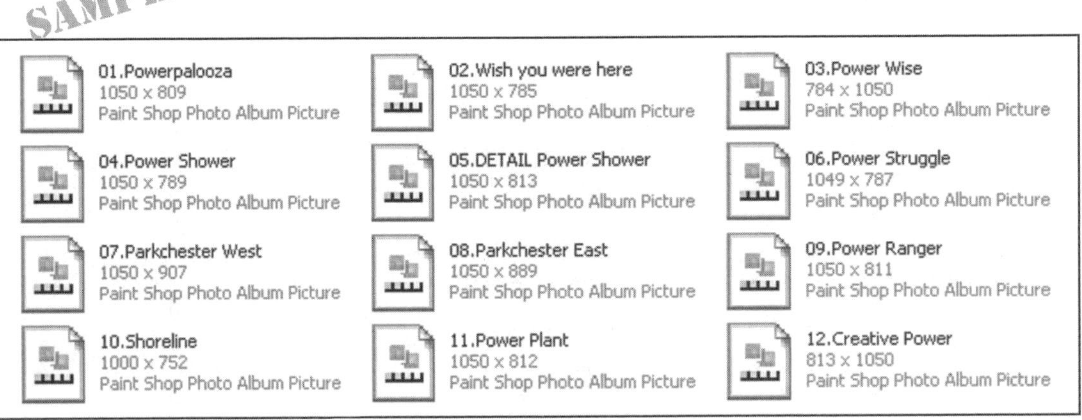

If you number the images *1.Title, 2.Title,* etc., the image labeled "10" will appear before the image labeled "1" on your disk.

The list is easy to read.

The information should be provided in a consistent order.

If you start with the title of the work and then list the year, media, dimensions, and price, stay with that sequence every time.

A detail shot should immediately follow the photograph of the entire artwork.

Label details clearly.

Example:
04. Power Shower
05. DETAIL Power Shower

The artwork dimensions are presented consistently.

- If you're sending a packet to a venue in the United States, list the dimensions of your artwork in inches. **Order the dimensions in this sequence: height by width by depth.** Don't include depth for two-dimensional work. Even if the two-dimensional work is created on a panel that is five inches deep, do not include the depth. An exception is if the work is a wall-hung work with wires and baubles protruding into the room from the piece. Use common sense here.
- If your work is framed and the frame adds a foot or more to the art, list a framed and an unframed size. For juried shows, always send the framed size. For galleries, grants, and publications, send the unframed size.

Describe the media in more detail, if applicable.

The image list gives you an opportunity to list all the media used to create the piece. If your work is made up of acrylic paint, collage, rubber stamping, color pencil, and pressed flowers on paper, don't just write mixed media.

List the ingredients of your art just as a cereal box does, putting the most-used media first and the least-used at the end. However, list no more than six or seven items. If your work is acrylic on panel, then that's all that's needed.

TITLE	YEAR	MEDIA	DIMENSIONS
1. *Power Ranger*	2006	Acrylic, ink, stickers on panel	28"h x 36"w
2. *Power Towers*	2005	"	36"h x 28"w
3. DETAIL, *Power Towers*			
4. *Power Happy*	2006	"	24"h x 24"w
5. *Power Play 2*	2006	"	24"h x 24"w
6. *Power Plant*	2006	"	28"h x 36"w
7. *Love is in the Air*	2006	"	20"h x 16"w
8. *Power Flower*	2005	"	36"h x 28"w
9. *Fancy Free*	2006	"	24"h x 36"w
10. *Power Play 3*	2006	"	24"h x 36"w
11. *Power Wise*	2007	"	48"h x 36"w
12. *Powerpalooza*	2007	"	36"h x 48"w
13. *Power Struggle*	2007	"	48"h x 36"w
14. *Power Shower*	2007	"	36"h x 48"w

Detailed list in table format.

Be cautious if you don't title your work.

If all your work is untitled, you will have a more difficult time keeping track of your work for inventory and acceptance into exhibitions.

I suggest naming untitled works as *Untitled 1, Untitled 2,* etc. I also suggest sending an image list with thumbnails. Always keep a copy for your records. It's not professional to be confused over which works you submitted for an exhibition.

TITLE	YEAR	MEDIA	DIMENSIONS
1. *Power Shower* 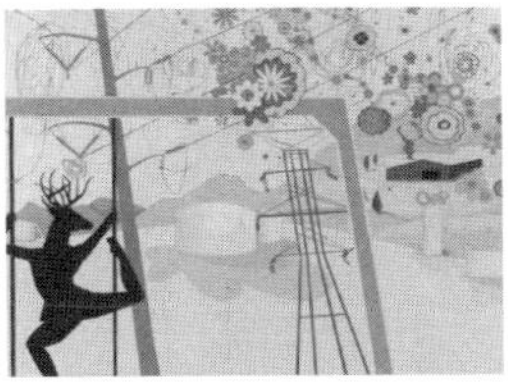 This body of work is meant to convey the play of energy generated between the industrial and natural elements of the landscape. I behold and appreciate the industrial for its atypical beauty while aware of its implications on nature.	2008	Acrylic and latex on panel	36"h x 48"w
2. *Power Shower* DETAIL			
3. *Power Struggle* 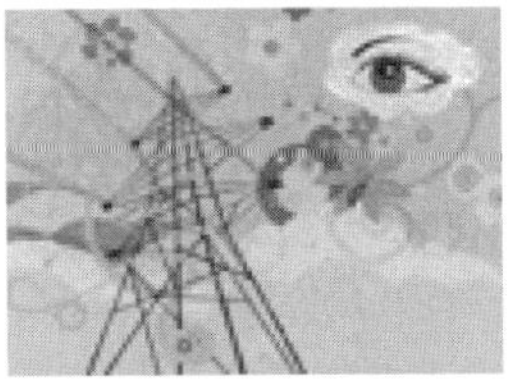 Power lines that come in an assortment of configurations remind me of stoic totem poles, carnival rides and human personalities. These structures rise up from the landscape next to sand dunes, blue heron and the lake.	2008	Acrylic and latex on panel	36"h x 48"w
4. *Wish You Were Here* 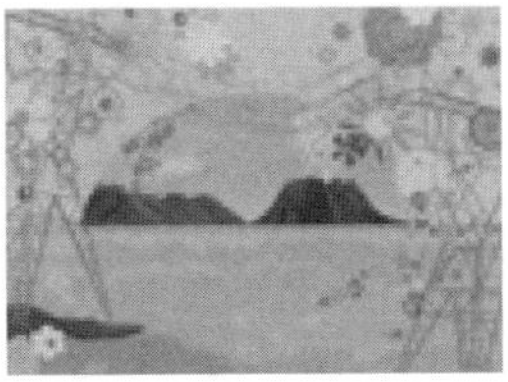 Mingling reality and whimsy, I create my own narratives and symbolize unseen forces such as electrical power and genetics with swirling paint. The paint swirling is an inherently spontaneous process that I then subvert by laying down rigorous, industrial forms to give the painting structure.	2009	Acrylic and latex on panel	36"h x 48"w
4. *Parkchester West* 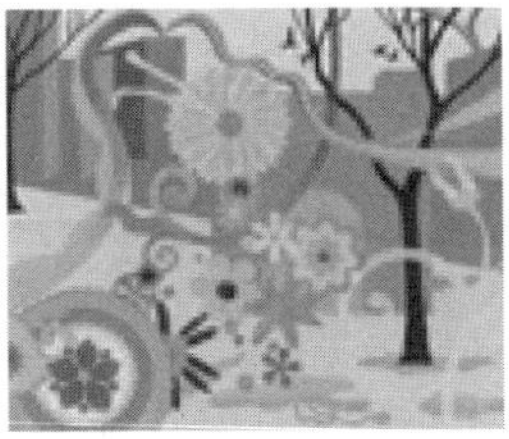 This was a finalist entry for a window design for a transit station in The Bronx. It was meant to celebrate The Bronx as a "melting pot." To illustrate the diversity of the community I utilized floral patterns imbued with cultural references that sometimes overlay and meld together.	2008	Gouache on board	21"h x 21"w

Annotated image list.

Sometimes guidelines request that you send an annotated image list. This is a list that has a thumbnail of each work as well as a brief explanation of each piece. For example, public art submissions ask you to describe the location of a work and the commissioning agency. You might also include one or two sentences about the project.

I was recently asked by a nonprofit institution to send an image list that also provided thumbnail images of each work I was submitting on my disk. This is helpful to the juror, curator, or panel in identifying exactly which work they're looking at on your disk and will ensure there's no confusion.

Assignment: *Create an image list and burn a compact disk with the images that correspond correctly to the list.*

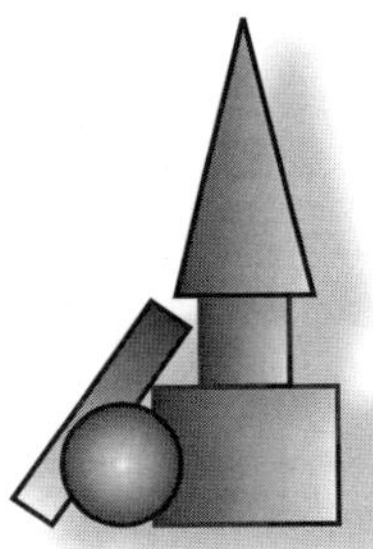

Chapter 5 *The Artist's Résumé*

Just as you need a résumé to look for a job, you also need a résumé to include in the packet you send to galleries. The purpose of an art résumé is to communicate the highlights of an artist's accomplishments.

Résumés are required of an artist for a variety of purposes. In this workbook I'll help you compose a résumé you can use for many opportunities, such as looking for gallery representation and applying for grants and residencies. A résumé that an artist creates to look for a particular job is different from the art-related résumé I'll help you develop here. I'll discuss a job résumé at the end of this chapter.

When I teach workshops, I always get résumé questions that reflect artists' insecurities about where they are in their career and what they've accomplished. Such questions include "What if I didn't go to art school?" and "What if I don't have any awards?"

Relax! Most artists begin their careers with very little experience. The important thing is to go forward now and develop your professional accomplishments. Accept the place where you are and proceed from there. You can develop quite an impressive résumé in just a year or two.

Developing Your Résumé

To develop your résumé, you must look for opportunities. There are several publications and websites that list opportunities for artists, such as juried competitions and grants. These opportunities are often referred to as calls for art. At the end of this book, I've compiled a resource list of my favorites and ones that other artists I know have found beneficial. This is by no means a comprehensive list.

If you don't have an exhibition history, this is where you should focus first. Look to begin showing your work locally and regionally. Start by seeking opportunities that match the type of work you do in content, style, or medium. If, for example, you're an emerging photographer and your subject matter is adolescents coming of age, then I'd look for:

- Local and regional calls for art that are exclusively for photography
- Local, regional, and national calls that emphasize a thematic content of portraiture, coming of age, or other topics that ring a true chord with your subject matter
- Local and regional works on paper calls that include photography

Works on paper refers to artwork that is made of or on paper and includes drawings, prints, and paper sculptures. Photography is sometimes excluded from this genre and given its own category.

Note that I left out several types of calls, including local, regional, and national open exhibition calls (no specific theme or media) and national photography shows. Of course, I encourage you to apply to any shows you have a good feeling about, but the latter types usually attract hundreds of entries. All shows are competitive, but at this tender stage I want you to spend your energy and money where they will likely have more impact.

Think of building a logical career trajectory. Show as much as you can at the local and regional level. Join arts organizations in your area that are well respected. Find out if they have members' shows or other exhibitions where you can gain exposure. You want to build local name recognition and your résumé.

Organizing Your Art Résumé

Here are some tips for creating your résumé. See the model on page 33 for an example of a standard one-page résumé to be included in a packet submitted to galleries.

For most uses, keep your résumé to one page.

Most of you at the beginning of your career will breathe a sigh of relief and think, "No problem!" In the next chapter, I'll give instructions for designing a résumé for beginners that doesn't look bare.

Again, I reiterate that I'm making suggestions for creating a résumé geared to pursuing art opportunities rather than the résumé that is used for job-hunting. When a résumé is required for grant and residency applications, the artist may be one of hundreds applying for these opportunities. So no matter how extensive your experience is, it's important for you to filter out the highlights and present them on one page. You don't want the reader to have to sift through your less important accomplishments, because there is a good chance he or she won't see the gems. I've read résumés that buried solo shows, prizes, and other highlights in a sea of miscellaneous experiences—and had I not specifically looked for these honors, I would have missed them.

When a résumé isn't vetted for your best endeavors, there's also the danger of communicating that you're naïve about the art world. You show a lack of knowledge about the professional landscape if you lump a show at the local coffee shop in with a small museum show. I'll explain this in more detail in this chapter under Editing Your Résumé.

Never put a picture of yourself on your résumé.

You don't want people making judgments about you based on your looks or age.

There's no need to title the résumé with the word "Résumé."

Everyone will know they're looking at your résumé if you create it properly.

Contact Information

All résumés, whether a hard copy (a printout) or on your website, should contain your name, home address, telephone number, and e-mail address. Don't list more than one address, e-mail account, or phone number. Just put the phone number at which someone is most likely to reach you or be able to leave you a message. Website addresses are optional. If you have a website that is complete and you are proud of, then include it.

Organize in Descending Order

Organize the dates of degrees, shows, grants, publications, and so on from the most recent year to earlier years.

Basic Categories of Information

Described below are the basic categories of information included in most art résumés. The rule of thumb is that except for Education, in order to justify making a separate category, there should be a minimum of two entries.

Education

You can place the Education category first or last. I prefer it first. If you went to many different universities, I suggest listing no more than three. Always list the school(s) where you received your degree(s).

List your degrees whether or not they are art-related. Having a degree in nursing or an MBA is still relevant in an art résumé. If you have no college background, then leave Education off your résumé. Please don't list every place you've ever taken an art lesson or attended a workshop. This usually looks like an artist is trying to make up for feelings of inadequacy. Art school is important and can be impressive, but it isn't necessary for an artist's success. I know many successful artists who never spent a day in art school.

A word about dates

Artists who graduated a while back (this varies from 10 to 50 years ago) often ask me if they have to include the year of their degree in their résumé. No, you don't have to. However, what would you infer from a résumé with no years listed under Education? Most people will infer that the person is old, perhaps much older than the artist actually is. My personal conclusion is that the artist is insecure with who he or she is and, for me, it's essential that the résumé convey confidence. So beware of such decisions. They are yours to make, but they convey ideas about you that you may not intend.

Solo Exhibitions

For exhibition entries, I wouldn't go back further than 20 years. However, you need to use some common sense here. If you were in a prestigious exhibition such as the Whitney Biennial in 1988, then by all means include this on your résumé forever. But some artists are unrealistically attached to their every accomplishment. I've tried to convince clients to let go of a 20-year-old group show in a gallery that no longer exists. Move forward!

If you have only one solo show, don't make a separate category for solo exhibitions. It looks silly to create a separate category for one entry. The challenge is to place the entry under Selected Exhibitions in such a way that the accomplishment doesn't get lost. This can be achieved by setting the words "solo exhibition" in a bolder typeface or in all capital letters. However, don't get carried away and make it so bold or different that it looks out of place. Try out a few different ideas and get the opinion of someone with a design background.

Selected Exhibitions

This section comprises all group shows in which you've exhibited work, including two- and three-person exhibitions. You can highlight two- and three-person shows in the same way you indicate a solo show if you don't have a separate Solo Exhibitions category. Use either all capital letters or boldface or italics. Do not create a separate category for two- and three-person shows.

Invitational? Juried?

An **invitational exhibit** is one in which the artists are invited to participate by the organizer or curator, based on knowledge of their artwork.

A **juried show** is a competition that's open to a large pool of artists (there may be no restrictions or some restrictions, such as geographical) and judged by one person or more.

Invitational exhibits and juried shows can be combined in this category. The judges' credentials vary widely and may range from community members, educators, and artists to museum curators or art critics. There's no need to indicate this distinction on your résumé, except in cases where you want to include the name of the juror. Most of the time, a juror's name is important to include on your résumé only if he or she is a collector, critic, curator, or famous artist. For the most part, you won't include the names of jurors who are professors and/or local (that is, not nationally known) artists. Most people reading your résumé won't be familiar with these people and so their credentials will not be meaningful to the reader. I don't mean to diminish these shows or these jurors; I am pointing out that using their names on your résumé won't open doors for you.

However, if the juror is a curator of even a very small museum, this does lend credibility. Since most of us don't know the names of curators around the world, you will want to indicate both the name and title of this type of juror on your résumé.

EXAMPLE:

2009 Contemporary Painting, ABC Gallery, Chicago, IL
juried by Jane Smith, curator of the Harris-Hawkins Museum, Springfield, IL

Awards and Grants

Use this category to list grants, relevant scholarships, fellowships, show prizes, and residencies. Include exhibition awards such as Best of Show, First Prize, and Second Prize. For Third Prize, Honorable Mention, and Merit Award, I would simply replace each with the phrase "Juror's Award." It's still true but sounds a lot better.

If the prize you won has a very long name that doesn't indicate the level of the award, I'd change it on the résumé. For example, South Shore Arts in Munster, Indiana, gives an award every year called the Helen V. Surovek Memorial Award. This is the top show prize, but unless your readers are very familiar with South Shore Arts in Munster, Indiana, they won't know that. It's by no means a stretch to put Best of Show on your résumé if you win this award.

Residencies are awards that afford artists the opportunity to live and create their work at facilities such as estates or campgrounds either free of charge or for a nominal fee. Some residencies last a few days and some are six months. A few even pay the artist a stipend. Artists compete for these opportunities, so they are considered awards and should be listed in this section.

Collections

In this section you should list public and private institutions, corporations, and major public figures who own your work. You may list libraries, universities, hospitals, restaurants, and businesses. You should also list well-known collectors such as the Pritzkers (of Chicago) and Leonardo DiCaprio. Do not list the names of all the family members, friends, and neighbors who own your work. This information is meaningless to the readers of your résumé.

Publications

What you list in this section depends in large part on where you are in your art career. If you're starting out, you may include poetry journals or university publications that have published your art. There is a prestigious annual book many artists have been juried into called New American Paintings. This publication and similar art magazines would be appropriate to list. However, I do not think that publications the artist pays to be part of should be included. This is equivalent to an advertisement and is not appropriate for a résumé.

If you are further along in your career, this would be the place to list feature articles or reviews about your work. Follow a consistent bibliography format that includes the author, name of the publication, issue number, and date. You can also opt to include actual articles and reviews in your packet. Copy each onto an 8½" x 11" sheet of paper and label it with the name of the publication and the date. Then scan the article into your computer and copy it onto the submission disk. Highlight the section of the article or review that is about your work. Don't include reviews of group shows or list them on your résumé if they don't specifically mention you or your work.

Mature artists may have quotations, paragraphs, or even chapters of books devoted to their work. Obviously, such distinctions will displace smaller accomplishments. As many art publications and major newspapers go out of business, a multitude of art-related websites are popping up. Many of these are legitimate sources for reviews, and some carry a lot of cachet. You may include these under publications as well.

Things that don't belong in this section are calendar listings, postcards, blurbs about you on your best friend's blog, reprinted press releases, and a photograph published in a paper or magazine for gallery publicity purposes. This is merely a news listing.

Janet Bloch | 497 Highland Drive, Chesterton, IN 46304 | 219-926-8318

janetbloch@verizon.net

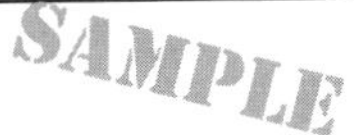

EDUCATION

MFA 1980	School of the Art Institute of Chicago—Chicago, IL
BFA 1978	School of the Art Institute of Chicago—Chicago, IL

SOLO EXHIBITIONS

2009	South Shore Arts—Munster, IN
2008	Linda Warren Gallery—Chicago, IL
2004	Gescheidle—Chicago, IL
2002	Woman Made Gallery—Chicago, IL
	Grand Street Window Project—Phoenix, AZ
2000	LyonsWier Packer Gallery—Chicago, IL
1999	LyonsWier Gallery—Chicago, IL
1998	Sioux City Art Center—Sioux City, IA
1997	LyonsWier Gallery—Chicago, IL

SELECTED EXHIBITIONS

2008	*Currents,* Studio Montclair—Montclair, NJ
	(Juried by Beth Venn, curator of Newark Museum)
2007	*Flatlands –Imaging the Midwest,* South Bend Regional Museum of Art—South Bend, IN
2006	*ART CHICAGO,* Merchandise Mart—Chicago, IL
	Nova Art Fair, Belmont Suites Hotel—Chicago, IL
2005	*SOFA Chicago,* Navy Pier—Chicago, IL
2003	ART CHICAGO, Navy Pier—Chicago, IL
	A.I.R. Gallery 5th Biennial —New York, NY
	(Juried by Shamim Momim, Curator, Whitney at Altria)
2001	*Nine State Open,* Sioux City Art Center—Sioux City, IA—First Prize
	(Juried by Dr. Henry Adams, Curator of American Painting, Cleveland Museum of Art)
2000	*International 2000,* San Diego Art Institute—San Diego, CA
1998	*College of Lake County* (two person show)—Grayslake, IL

AWARDS & GRANTS

2009, 2006	Individual Artist's Grant—Indiana Arts Commission
2008	Finalist—New York MTA Metro Art, public art design for a subway station
2007	Finalist—Los Angeles Metro Art, public art design for a subway station
2005	Juror's Award—*Salon Show* juried by Karl Wirsum, Northern Indiana Arts Assoc.
2001	First Prize—*Nine State Open,* Sioux City Art Center, Iowa
1997	Grant—Illinois Arts Council, Visual Artists Fellowship
1996	Grant—Arts Midwest/NEA Regional, Visual Artists Fellowship
1996, 95, 91	Grant—Community Artists Assistance Program, Chicago Department of Cultural Affairs

COLLECTIONS

Appalachian State University—Boone, NC
Deloitte—Chicago, IL
Sioux City Art Center—Sioux City, IA
South Bend Regional Museum of Art—South Bend, IN

PUBLICATIONS

Harper's Magazine—February 1999
New American Paintings #17, Open Studios Press—1998

Editing Your Résumé

As you begin to use the strategies set forth in this book, you'll start building your résumé. Each time you show your work, add that information. Eventually, you'll get to a point where you have more than a page. Here are some pointers to guide you in continuing to edit your résumé down to one page.

Let's say you've been showing your work in your geographical area for a few years now and that you have been in the annual Members' Show at ABC Gallery every year for the last four years. Guess what? There's too much ABC Gallery on your résumé. It's time to get your work out of town. You need to diversify your résumé once you've begun to develop it. So after you've built your résumé a bit, look through it for exhibitions that gave prizes, were out of state or in big cities, had important jurors, or were held in museums. You will want to keep most of these. Replace shows in cafés with shows in bigger institutions or galleries. Take off the member shows, student shows, alumni exhibits, and shows from your guild or society and replace them with more prestigious and diverse shows in order to build your credentials. Change the head for this section of your résumé from Juried Exhibitions to Selected Juried Exhibitions.

The Work Résumé

A résumé created to apply for a job is very different from the résumé you use to present your artistic endeavors. Of course, there will be overlap if you're seeking an art-related position. Activities such as curating exhibitions, writing articles, jurying shows, and serving on boards are all experiences you could include on a work résumé, depending on the position you're seeking. Describe the responsibilities and accomplishments you attained in previous positions that are related to the position you're seeking. If you're applying for a teaching post, it's a good idea to put a description of classes you've taught. There are many books on how to create an excellent job-seeking résumé. Since this isn't my area of expertise, I refer you to the Internet for a wealth of free information on this topic.

Assignment: *Create a one-page résumé for yourself or a fellow artist. Make sure all the formatting is consistent.*

Chapter Notes

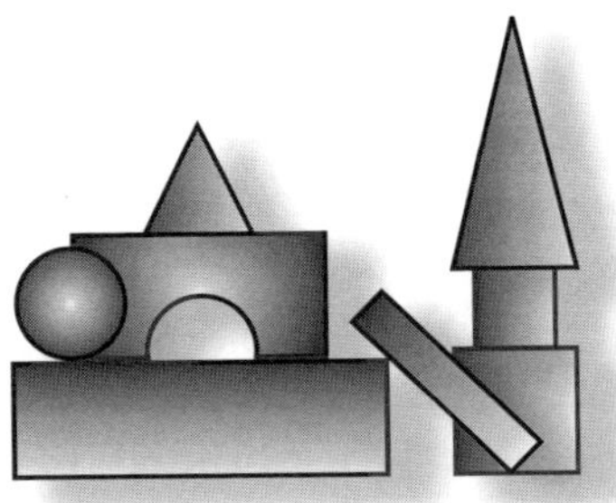

Chapter 6 *Designing Your Résumé*

If a résumé isn't easy to read, it isn't successful. This doesn't mean it can't be beautifully designed and creative. However, I will caution you that taking too much creative license on a résumé (or business card or other marketing materials) can backfire. For most artists, I suggest concentrating on creating a clean, readable document without fancy type or logos. There was a time I would have said never use a logo, because the art world has its prejudices against "designers" as opposed to artists. However, many young artists have convinced me otherwise. If you use a logo, make certain that it ties in with the artwork you make and so establishes you and your work as a brand.

In creating a brand, you are communicating to your audience that they can trust your product (your art) to have certain unique qualities or characteristics. This tool can be very useful in promoting your work to the public, especially if you have a product that can be mass-marketed. A few clever artists will be able to create value and demand for their work by careful branding. However, branding is not a tool that all artists will want to utilize. For many artists, narrowing the scope of their artwork to meet their audience's expectations is too constricting. It may defeat the idea of the artist's role in society as that of someone who is always creating something unexpected and original.

Many artists won't pull off branding successfully. In some ways, the art world subscribes to conservative conventions, and unless this type of marketing is truly suited to your work, it's best to save your originality for your artwork.

When printed (as opposed to digitally sent or posted to a website), all résumés should be on simple, tasteful paper that both looks and feels high-quality.

The All-in-One

If you're just starting out and have little professional experience, I have a format that works well. You obviously don't want to send out a résumé with a half-empty page, nor do you want to use 36-point type. Therefore, I suggest using a format I call the all-in-one. It includes:

- Your contact information
- A crisp image of one of your artworks, preferably a more graphic piece. By graphic, I mean an image that is easily understood because it has good contrast and reproduces with clarity.
- A brief artist's statement
- Any professional experience you have

The key to a successful all-in-one is that it communicates confidence. It should be nicely designed and contain concise information. The reader will not focus on your lack of experience but rather on your finesse.

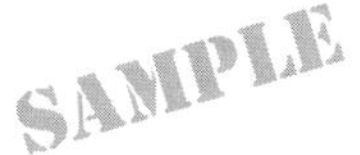

BEATRICE FISHER

1234 Main Street Evanston, Il. 00000 123-000-000 beatricef@xxx.com

EDUCATION

B.A. in English and Theatre, Wayne State University, Detroit, MI

SELECTED EXHIBITIONS

2009 *And You think That's Funny*, Woman Made Gallery, Chicago, IL
juried by Nicole Hollander, artist, creator of *Sylvia*

2008 *Rockford Midwestern*, Rockford Art Museum, Rockford, IL

AWARDS

2009 4 Week Residency, Ragdale Foundation, Lake Forest, IL
2008 4 Week Residency, Vermont Studio Center, Johnson, VT
Juror's Award, *Rockford Midwestern*, Rockford Art Museum, Rockford, IL
2007 2 Month Painting Residency, Anderson Ranch Arts Center, Snowmass, Colorado

This current series of artwork reflects my interest in incongruous psychological states. I investigate themes of childhood, aging, love, separation and loss. My style and sensibilities are influenced by Magritte, the Chicago Imagists and Outsider Art. In similar ways, I have interest in depicting illogical narratives. My intent is to make the work both humorous and dark, with a penchant for ambiguity and the absurd.

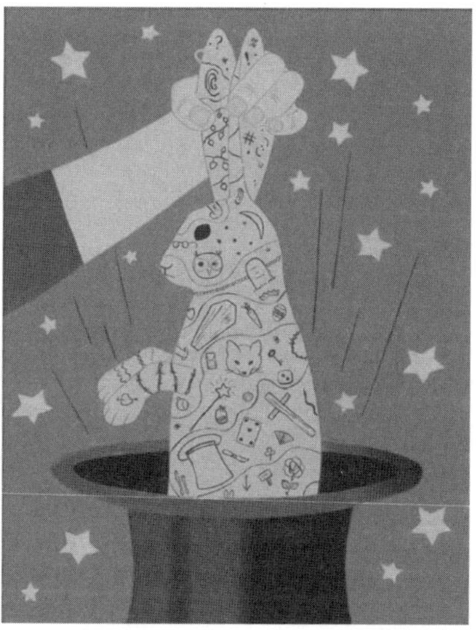

Blue Rabbit, 2008, acrylic on panel, 16" x 12"

Formatting Your Résumé

I suggest using a maximum of two typefaces for most résumés. Then use point size, capital letters, italics, or bold type to differentiate the information. The hierarchy of the entries should be easy to follow, and this requires consistency in formatting. In listing your entries, make sure you follow the same sequence every time. A good formula for listing an exhibition entry is the year, title of the exhibit, venue of the exhibit, city, state, and juror (if important enough to warrant inclusion). Another key to cleaning up the look and legibility of a résumé is to list the year in the left margin once and then indent all the entries for that year.

Type Talk

Point: 1/72nd of an inch

Pica: 12 points, 1/6th of an inch

Inch: 72 points or 6 picas (typographer's inch)

5.5 point (agate) used in classified ads

8 point

9 point

10 point

11 point

12 point

14 point

Type is measured from the top of an ascender like a lower case "l" or "h" to the bottom of a lower case descender like a "y" or "p". The capital is about 2/3 of the point size.

2010	*The Greatest Show on Earth,* ABC Gallery, Chicago, IL
	All About Me, Awesome Museum of Art, New York, NY *Juried by Jane Doe, Critic, New Yorker*
	Painting for Your Life, Center for the Best Painters, Anytown, IN
2009	*Health and Beauty,* XYZ Gallery, Waytogo, OH
	Prosperity Now, Bloch Center for the Arts, Metropolis, NY

Personally, I believe the type size should never be smaller than 8 or 9 points. My graphic designer friends vehemently disagree. All I can say is that if your audience can't read it, even if it looks cool, you're in trouble.

Biography (Bio)

A biography is simply your résumé composed in a narrative form. It's written in the third person, as opposed to an artist statement, which is always written in the first person.

A bio is like the blurb about an author on a book jacket—and, in fact, you will find mine on the back cover of this workbook.

Generally, you don't send a bio as part of your submission packet for fine art opportunities. You'll need one for flyers and/or class catalogs if you teach workshops or give presentations. You'll also want one when you send out a press release about an exhibition, product, or workshop you're presenting. Always highlight your professional achievements in a biography and give some specific examples.

Don't just say:

Jane Doe has received many awards for her work nationally.

Change to:

Jane Doe has received many awards for her work nationally, including an Illinois Arts Council grant and a Guggenheim Foundation Fellowship.

Sometimes a bio will contain a small bit of personal information. The appropriateness of this information depends on where the bio will be used. For example, if you're giving a talk at a local garden club on your recent series of botanical prints, your bio may include something about your own interest in gardening as a hobby.

Sample Bio

Janet Bloch earned a Master of Fine Arts from the School of the Art Institute of Chicago. Bloch is the recipient of numerous grants, including an Illinois Arts Council Visual Artists Fellowship and an NEA Regional/Midwest Fellowship. A three-time grantee of the Community Artists Assistance Program from the Chicago Department of Cultural Affairs, she also has extensive experience giving professional workshops for artists interested in exhibiting their work. Bloch has had several solo exhibits nationwide, and her work has been featured at several Chicago art fairs, such as SOFA on Navy Pier, ART CHICAGO, and NOVA. To see samples of Bloch's work, go to *www.janetbloch.womanmade.net.*

Assignment: *Create an all-in-one if your experience is limited.*

Assignment: *Create a biography for yourself.*

Chapter Notes

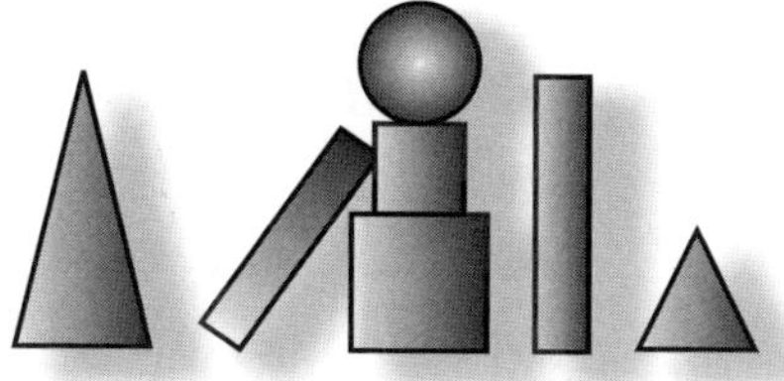

Chapter 7 *The Artist's Statement*

The purpose of your artist's statement is to communicate, in a concise and direct way, what you investigate, observe, or want to express with your art. This is accomplished by informing the reader about specific motives, processes, and influences.

Many artists have a difficult time writing their statement, but it's a very good exercise for figuring out exactly who you are as an artist and what you hope to convey through your work. If you exhibit your work mainly at art fairs or in artisan galleries, a statement that focuses on your process (how you make your art) may suffice.

However, if you intend to enter the fine art world and be taken seriously, you must develop your artist statement fully. The notion that the statement is merely an academic exercise that is full of "art speak" is outdated. As you embark on your art career, you'll be expected to discuss the ideas your art addresses with your audience, other artists, collectors, curators, and critics. Of course, you want to be able to articulate your vision in these discussions.

Writing a statement will help you do just that. Whatever your objections, please suspend them for now. The statement will not limit your options or stifle your creativity. Set aside your resistance, because I'm going to help you write a useful and powerful statement that will tell the world who you are as an artist.

The first mistake many artists make is to launch into writing a statement before taking the time to journal about their work. Below is a list of exercises that I suggest you take some time to complete before starting your statement. My advice is to answer each question over the next few weeks. Not every question will resonate with you about your work, but answer all of them anyway. For example, if you're a painter with a fairly traditional technique, your statement need not mention your process, but journal about it first to make sure you're not overlooking an interesting detail.

If a question resonates with you, return to it several times. Allow yourself to delve deeper into the topic each time. If you find it difficult to discipline yourself, set a timer for ten minutes and write until the time is up. Over time, information and insights will emerge about your work. I suggest writing without formality at this stage. Don't get hung up on grammar and punctuation, as you can polish your writing later in the process. Following are several questions that will help you begin to formulate your statement.

Writing Exercises

1. ***What are the two most important themes (ideas, concepts) that your artwork addresses?***

loss, creating ~~objects~~ images to look real at 1st glane
play w/ ideas of relegion, + sexuality.
opression of women, sickness + death,

2. ***What are the two greatest influences (genres of art, artists, philosophies, etc.) on your current work? Explain the relationship of each to your work.***

hold on to things lost ie childhood, love, family, ideas, dreams, memories, objects

3. ***Describe, step by step, your entire process for creating an artwork.***

4. ***List five words or phrases that describe your art. Examples: layered, flat, narrative, congested, complex, adorned.***

1.

2.

3.

4.

5.

5. ***Ask three friends (artists and nonartists) to list five words or phrases that describe your art.***

6. ***What is your motivation? Be specific. Don't use the words personal and universal. Complete the following sentences:***

The intent of this body of work is

7. ***How do you decide where to go with a piece while you're creating it?***

My aesthetic decisions are informed by

8. ***I think my best works have (what qualities)***

9. ***I envision my work developing (in what ways)***

10. ***If I were going to be as gutsy as possible with the creation of my artwork, I would***

____

____

____

____

____

Assignment: Journal on all the exercises above over the next several weeks.

While you're busy journaling, let's continue to learn more about how to write an artist's statement. Following is a list of do's and don'ts with specific examples to make sure you understand the concepts.

Do's and Don'ts

Do write your statement in the first person ("I" statements).

This is your declaration of what your art is about. Make it a natural extension of your work.

Do keep your statement fairly brief.

A good statement includes the essential ideas behind your art. However, you may write variations on your statement for different purposes. For example, a grant application might request that you discuss any historical traditions your artwork is based on. This may not be one of the prevalent influences in your art and therefore not part of your core statement. Nevertheless, you'll have to address it in your grant application.

A good length for a statement is two paragraphs, 150 to 200 words total. (If you use Microsoft Word, you can use the Tools/Word Count function to see how long your statement is.) One paragraph is too short unless a guideline specifically requests that you submit only one paragraph. Unless a longer statement is requested or a specific word limit is given, the maximum anyone wants to read is three paragraphs, or approximately 300 words.

Don't be generic in your assertions.

If what you write can be said about most artists or artwork, you need to be more specific. Write about the particular works you're exhibiting or submitting, not about all the artwork you've ever produced. In fact, each body of artwork will require its own statement. Below are examples of generic statements:

BEFORE	AFTER
In allowing my paintings to become more personal, I hope they might become more universal.	The inability to change the circumstances in my daughter's life corresponds to a larger picture of being overwhelmed by the problems of humanity.
Within each painting are shifts of color with contrasts of light and dark, or softness and hardness of line.	I scrape, smooth, and incise layers of wax to build complexity and nuances of color and texture.

In the two "before" examples, I could be reading about the work of a thousand artists. The statements tell me nothing significant. You can see how striking the statements become when the artist is pushed to be more specific and make every word count.

Do keep sentence structure concise. Beware of rambling, confusing sentences.

BEFORE	AFTER
For me the process of creating art is a multilayered process of digging up archaic sensibilities and an invocation recalling the gods that have been relegated to the world of imagination, dreams, and fairy tales.	In my experience, the art-making process is an excavation of my inner wisdom, imagination, and spirit.

Don't combine two separate ideas in one sentence. Use one sentence for each idea.

I enjoy focusing on ephemeral moments and seek to preserve the character and uniqueness of the American streetscape and its environs.

Both of these ideas should be separated and expanded upon. They don't belong together in a sentence.

Don't repeat yourself.

Many artists say the same thing three different ways throughout their statements. If you state your point forcefully and clearly, you won't need to repeat it.

Do use active sentence structure.

Active sentence structure makes a stronger impact, and you will be less tempted to repeat your ideas.

BEFORE	AFTER
Ephemeral moments are focused on in my work.	I focus on ephemeral moments.
Investigating life's opposing elements is an area of interest for me.	I am interested in investigating life's opposing elements.

Do keep simplifying sentence structure.

BEFORE	AFTER
I am interested in investigating life's opposing elements.	I investigate life's opposing elements.

Don't be wishy-washy or dilute the meaning of your ideas.

Own your ideas. Get rid of conditional language such as *might, could, perhaps, probably,* and *seems.*

BEFORE	AFTER
It often seems to me . . .	I believe . . .

Don't set forth subjective statements as facts.

Presenting subjective statements (or opinions) as facts will set up an argumentative point of view with your audience. You can convey your philosophy, but reword it so that you own it.

BEFORE	AFTER
The world is fraught with danger and deception.	I see the world as fraught with danger and deception.
The documents of officialdom confine and define the bearer with a fixed identity and role.	In my exploration of identity, I inquire into the function of documents such as birth certificates, passports, and licenses.

Don't tell your audience what they see and feel or what your work achieves.

Again, this sets up an argumentative point of

view with your audience. Let the viewer decide if you're successful in achieving your intent.

BEFORE	AFTER
My use of bold color evokes passion.	I explore color for the psychological effects it produces.
My photographs sometimes have a sad, nostalgic, or lonely feel to them.	I often photograph abandoned places or discarded objects in order to convey a sense of loneliness.

Don't use obscure terms or references without explaining them.

If you use a term or reference that isn't widely known, briefly define it. Assume your audience is educated but may not have the time, opportunity, or energy to look up unfamiliar references. If a viewer is confused about your work, takes the time to read your statement, and then is further confused, he or she will feel angry and alienated. Your statement should enlighten the viewer.

BEFORE	AFTER
I use the theory of predictive encoding to examine ideas about evolution.	*Predictive encoding* is the term used to describe intuitively knowing that a piece of information will prove useful to one in the future. I investigate this phenomenon to examine ideas about evolution

Don't cite an influence without explaining your artworks' relationship to that inspiration.

You need to connect the dots for the viewer.

BEFORE	AFTER
I have found a kindred spirit in the painter Frida Kahlo.	In my use of text and personal iconography, I have found a kindred spirit in the painter Frida Kahlo.

Don't be flowery, poetic, or cutesy.

Your writing may sound pretty, but unless it enlightens the viewer regarding what your work is about, it doesn't belong in your statement. The effect may be that you sound corny. Make sure everything you write is authentic and has a purpose for being there. I suggest that your style be pithy rather than poetic. Remember that your artwork is your main venue for expressing yourself; the statement merely gives further insight.

Do read your statement out loud to yourself and others.

Read the statement to artists and nonartists to see if the language is accessible to many types of people. If, while reading aloud, you find the sentences or vocabulary difficult to manage, or if you feel pompous, embarrassed, or confused, revise your statement. Your statement should be a comfortable and authentic extension of you and your work.

Let others ask questions about your meaning and see if they've understood the message you're trying to convey. Do your ideas need more fleshing out?

Do understand that writing an artist's statement is a process.

You'll edit and revise your statement as your work and your understanding of your work grow. You also may have several statements for different purposes: one for grant applications, one for public art, and so on.

Assignment: *Research, write, then share your personal artist's statement.*

- **Step 1:** Find an artist's statement in a book or online and critique it specifically for the *do's* and *don'ts* given above.

- **Step 2:** After several weeks of journaling, write a first draft of your artist's statement.

- **Step 3:** Share your statement and images of your artwork with other artists and let them critique whether your statement truly reflects your work. Do the same for them in an honest yet constructive atmosphere. Revise your statement accordingly.

- **Step 4 (optional):** This exercise is beneficial to do in an artist's group. Each artist creates a statement that he or she is fairly happy with and then trades it with another artist. Each artist revises another's statement, utilizing the information in this chapter.

Chapter Notes

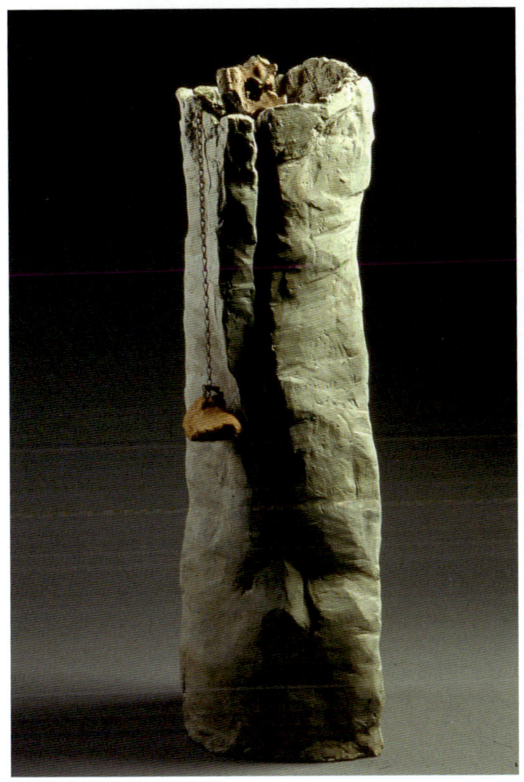

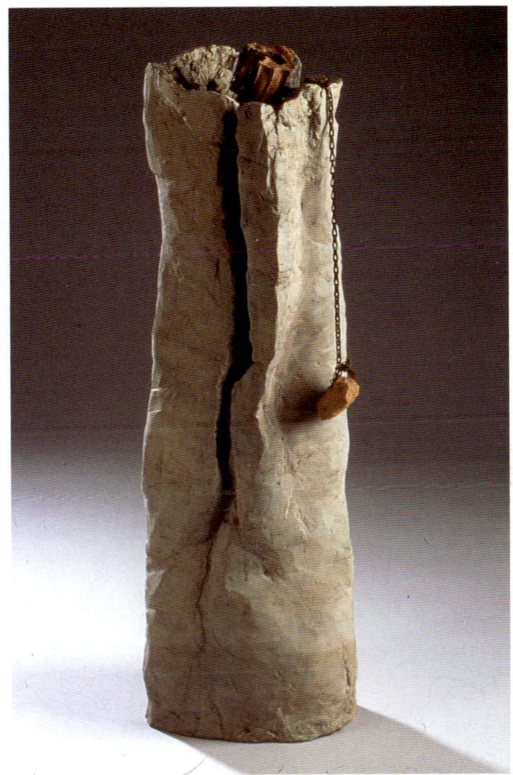

Photo credit: Cindy Trim

Illustration 1
Corinne D. Peterson: Moorings, terra cotta, chain, brick fragments, 35″ x 10″ x 8″

The photograph on the left is too dark and the incorrect use of lights alters the color of the sculpture. On the right, the photograph of the same piece is much more legible. The focus, lighting and positioning of the sculpture provides us with a wealth of information about the artist's technique and materials, resulting in a more compelling image.

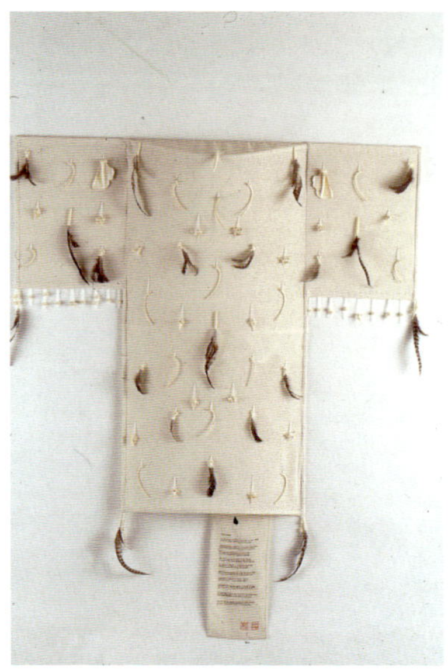

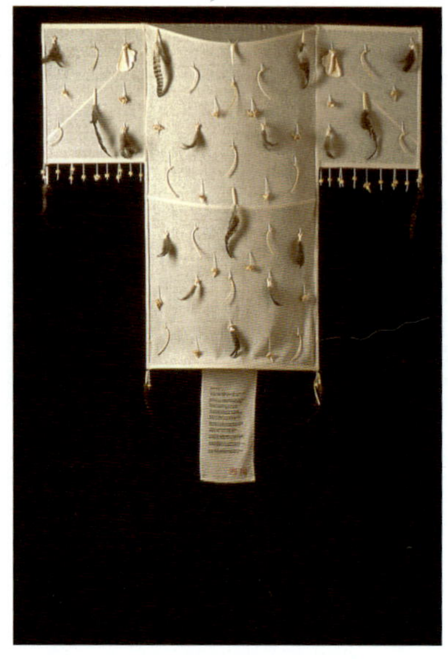

Photo credit: Cindy Trim

Illustration 2
Aimeé Picard, Kite, handwoven silk, wood, bones, feathers, and glass beads.
Text from "Flight Paths" with permission from poet Deena Linett, Collection of Marie and Emy Picard

In the photograph on the left, we are distracted from focusing on the artwork due to several elements, the first being the obviously crooked placement of the art in the photographic frame. The photograph is also out of focus, making it difficult to see the materials the artist used. The white background is a poor choice as the art blends in rather than stand out. On the right, the focus, backdrop choice of black, and the higher positioning of the art give drama and presence to the artwork.

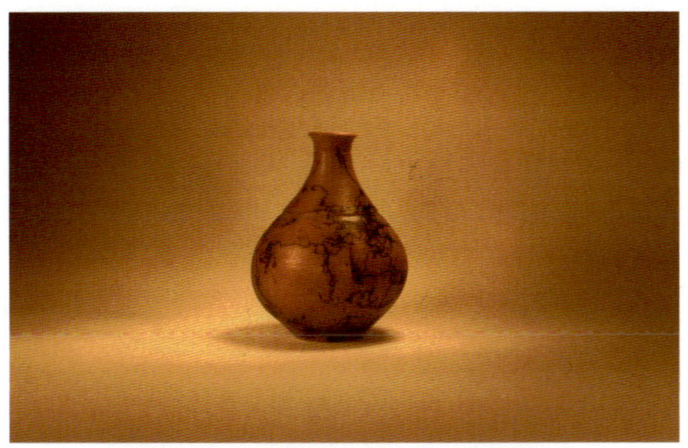

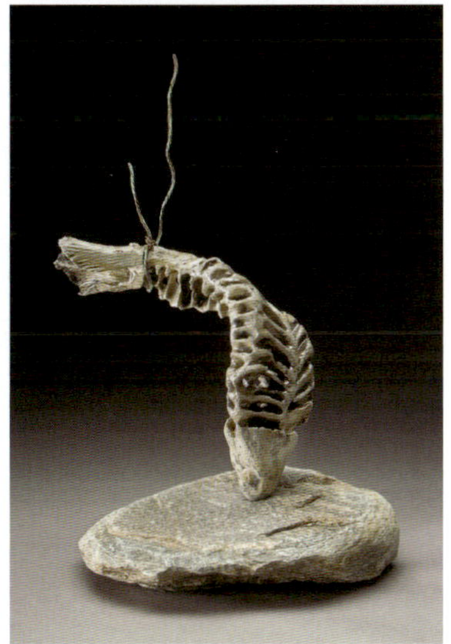

Photo Credit: Jay Bachemin

Illustration 3
Top: Artist Unknown
Bottom: Lisa Merida-Paytes, Frozen Fish on Granite, Raku, Granite, Copper Wire, 33″ x 24″ x 30″

In the top photograph the art piece is placed too small in the photographic frame. It would have been better to take the photograph with a vertical orientation and try to fill the frame with the artwork so we can see the surface detail of the vase. The photograph is also poorly lit and out of focus. The artwork is obscured by the poor choice of backgound color. The artwork on the bottom stands out beautifully against the background and the crisp focus and excellent placement of the sculpture let us focus on the artwork.

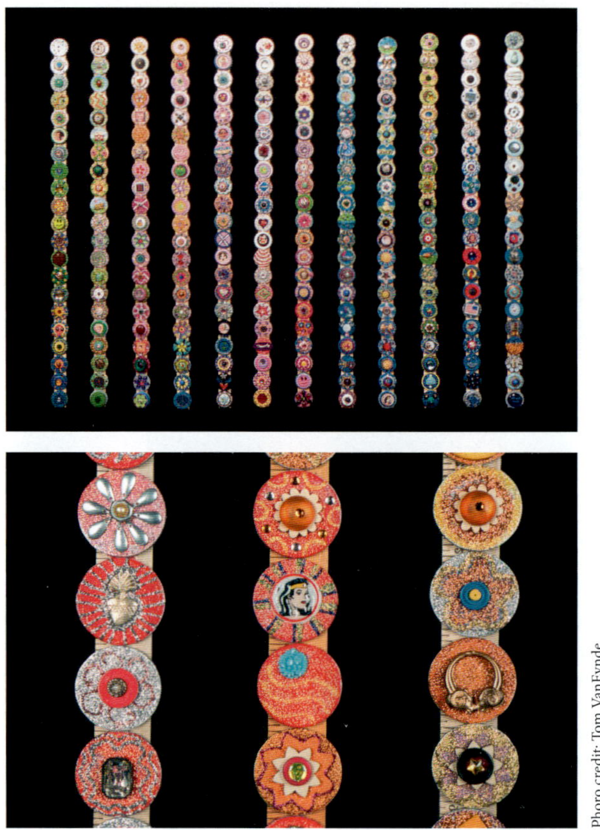

Phoro credit: Tom VanEynde

Illustration 4
Janet Bloch, Top: Sticks & Disks, yardsticks, wood disks, paint, stickers, notions, gems, etc., 36"h x 72"w.
Bottom: DETAIL, Sticks & Disks

The installation on the top produces certain color and design effects when viewed as a whole. Upon closer inspection the viewer can see the obsessive detail and variety of materials utilized, including many recycled items. In addition to a photograph of the whole art piece, a detail photograph is necessary to include in a submission for a complete understanding of the work of art. A detail shot needs to be well thought out and capture pertinent information, so that only one is needed.

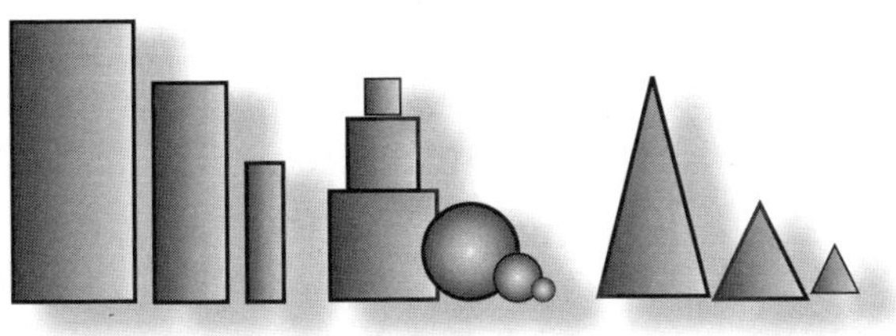

Chapter 8 *Research / Exploration*

If you have developed your résumé with lots of group exhibitions, created a body of work, and written an artist's statement, you are almost ready to send off a packet to introduce your work to a gallery or submit for a solo show opportunity at a nonprofit institution. But before you send off those proposals, you need to determine which exhibition places are truly a good match for your artwork. Therefore, I'm placing the research chapter of this workbook before the chapter on the cover letter and the exhibition proposal.

If You Can Visit

Many artists I meet want to show their work in a particular institution or gallery but do not make consistent efforts to visit or join those with memberships. This signals to me that an artist is looking for an opportunity that is "all get and no give." Don't make this mistake. Just as you wouldn't go to work for a company you were unfamiliar with or sign a contract with a business partner you don't know, you shouldn't send a proposal to an exhibition space without investigating it thoroughly.

I've heard artists groan when I suggest this. Try to alter your attitude by thinking of your research as traveling to visit the world's wondrous sites. Remember, as a traveler you would welcome the exploration of new places, read up on these spots before going to them, and anticipate the unfamiliar with excitement. You wouldn't get to the Grand Canyon and refuse to get out of the car, would you? Of course not! So let's continue our adventure with a traveler's curiosity and spirit.

If you live close to the gallery (in the same city or a suburb of it), I suggest that you see a minimum of six exhibitions there in a given year. If you do this, you'll know whether your work fits the gallery's direction. Following this advice doesn't mean you'll get your work into that gallery, but it will substantially increase the probability of doing so by demonstrating your interest, seriousness, and preparation.

Don't visit the gallery with the intention of talking to anyone about your work.

One mistake artists make is to go into a gallery for the first (or second) time and ask the gallery director if he or she is interested in, for example, exhibiting photography. If you've done your homework, you should know this already. Another mistake artists make is to go to a gallery with portfolio in hand, expecting someone to take the time to look at their work. This behavior signals ignorance about the workings of a gallery or institution, because the gallery directors and curators are busy and don't see people without appointments.

If you live in a city with galleries and don't attend them, you're being foolish. This will be confirmed by artists who don't live in areas with galleries, for if they had your access to the art world, they'd gladly show up.

Furthermore, consider the incongruity of not wanting to go to the exhibition space yet wanting the director to look at your art. This is self-centered behavior. When I directed Woman Made Gallery in Chicago, nothing turned me off more than an artist coming in and expecting me to view his or her portfolio without an appointment. Sometimes artists would call first and ask if

I'd look at their work.

Me:	*Are you a member of the Gallery? [There is a $35 yearly membership fee to belong to Woman Made.]*
Artist:	*No.*
Me:	*Have you been to Woman Made before?*
Artist:	*No, but I hear you show work by women.*
Me:	*Have you seen our website?*
Artist:	*No.*

I'd get off the phone politely but with the opinion that the artist was very naïve and selfish to do absolutely no investigation of the organization. It seemed it wasn't even worth the artist's time to come to the gallery unless I'd look at her work. These impressions stayed with me. While I believe it's unintentional on the artist's part and stems from a lack of knowledge about the art world, it's disrespectful, even arrogant, to behave in this manner. Please consider that the people in the business of showing artists' work have their own visions and goals.

So much can be learned by going to a gallery with an open mind and an earnest desire to learn about the gallery and the art exhibited there. Observe and think about the work that is on display. Study the craft, the style, the prices, and the concepts. If the average price of a 30" x 40" painting is $8,000 and you're an emerging artist, this gallery may not be a good match for you at this time. But you'll know this only if you attend consistently. One visit isn't enough to make a determination.

Answer the following questions every time you go to a gallery:

- ***What is the average price point for different media and different sizes?***
- ***How is the work presented?*** Specifically, if the work is two-dimensional, is it framed or not? How are works on paper presented?

  For instance, there is now a trend for edgier or younger galleries to exhibit drawings simply tacked up on the wall. Others present drawings only in pristine frames. Determine what material the frames are made of, what color is most prevalent, and so forth.

  The questions are endless:
- ***Are the paintings framed?***
- ***Are they on panels?***
- ***How are the sides of the paintings finished?***
- ***Are sculptures on pedestals?***
- ***What material are the pedestals made of?***

If the work is similar to yours, pay close attention and take notes. You may engage the gallery staff in questions if something is not apparent, but don't needlessly take their time with questions.

- ***What is the mood in the gallery? Were you acknowledged when you came in?***

Eventually, if you have a gallery representing your work, the relationship should be equal and mutual. You want to note the atmosphere of a gallery to see if you're comfortable with how the gallery staff treats the public.

When to visit the gallery

I believe it's useful to visit the gallery during its regular hours—when it's quiet—and also during openings. You'll have different learning experiences at each. At an opening you get to see what kind of following the gallery has developed. It's a great way to network as well. If you're shy, go with a friend who loves art. If you like the exhibition, set aside your shyness and make it a point to find the artist and tell him or her so.

Other artists as allies

Other artists are your best allies in this business. I'm part of a network of artists who help open doors for one another. Don't hesitate to be genuine and generous.

If an artist isn't receptive, don't take it personally. Sadly for them, this is their problem. You've done nothing wrong. Some people are snobbish, and that has nothing to do with the fact that they're an artist or that you have been inappropriate. Sometimes the artist is shy and has trouble chatting with strangers. Don't get discouraged if this happens, and never stop being gracious. Remember to treat people warmly when it's your opening!

Developing a rapport

When you visit the gallery during quieter, regular business hours, you'll have a better opportunity to focus on the work that's on display. I wouldn't be surprised if after three or four visits to a gallery, the owner or one of the staff members engages you in a conversation. If that happens and you are asked, it's fine to mention that you're an artist. You can say that you admire the gallery's programs and name a particular artist or show that stood out for you. Please follow the lead of the person you're talking to in terms of bringing up your own work. You'll have to become socially skilled at this.

Don't jump the gun and forcefully ask, "Can I show you my work?" You might undo your months of preparation in one minute. But the person might say, "I'd like to see your work sometime." A great answer is, "I'd be delighted to send you a packet. Do you review artists at a certain time of year?"

Do you see the confidence that comes from being knowledgeable?

If the person seems open to interaction, it's fine to show your enthusiasm. Whenever this type of conversation goes pleasantly, be sure to tell the person your name and say you'll send a packet. Then it's up to you to get that packet out in the next few days. Or to say, "I'm having a couple of new pieces photographed, and then I'll take you up on your generous offer."

A word about gallery staff members

Always be courteous and pleasant to them. If they don't like you, they'll prevent you from getting your work in front of the decision-makers. If they like you, they'll help you get your work seen. Always treat them with respect.

If You Can't Visit

Almost all the advice I've given you about visiting an exhibition space can be modified slightly for artists who live too far from the venue to visit in person. The way to apply this knowledge is to visit the website of the space consistently and "attend" exhibitions as a regular patron.

For instance, you can easily look up exhibitions that the venue has displayed in the last year. Most sites have extensive information about the artists they exhibit, including several images of each artist's work; each work's size, medium, and price; and each artist's résumé and statement. It could take months of good research to familiarize yourself with just six venues.

If a website doesn't have all this information, it's possible to run the names of various artists through an Internet search engine and find out more information about them. You may even be led to other venues where the artists show their work and investigate those places as well.

The only things you can't do on the Internet that you

can do by going to a gallery are experience the artwork in person and—just as important—meet the gallery personnel. I suggest visiting and researching the website a minimum of six times a year to examine the same issues I suggested for artists who can visit in person. At this stage you should know what elements and format the space requires for artist's submissions. Only then would I advise making contact, and the contact should be made in the format requested by the specific place.

Remember, whether you telephone or e-mail, always be patient and polite to the staff.

Assignment: *Visit one gallery in your area (or on the Internet if no galleries exist in your town) and take notes about the career level of the artists featured, the price point for artworks, the style of work exhibited, and so on. If you are able to visit in person, pay attention to the way the work is presented and how the staff treats you. Start a list of the places that you think you would like to exhibit your artwork down the road.*

Chapter Notes

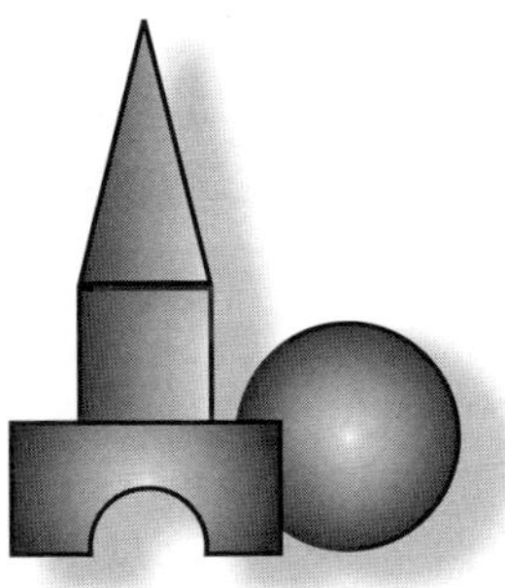

Chapter 9 *Cover Letters and Exhibition Proposals*

When you're ready to submit your materials for a solo show or gallery representation, a *cover lette*r serves as an introduction to the person to whom you're submitting materials. It isn't necessary to include a cover letter when you're applying to an institution, if the organization's guidelines don't request one. However, if you're sending materials to a gallery for consideration, you'll always want to include one. *Cover letters* are not required or needed when submitting your work to juried group exhibitions.

Exhibition proposals are usually required when submitting materials to institutions such as art centers and museums; they generally aren't required by a gallery. The cover letter and exhibition proposal differ in that the proposal may include information that pertains to an institution's mission and audience. It may also indicate how you would use the space in a site-specific manner.

Cover Letter

Always find the correct name and title of the person to whom you should address in your letter. Never send out a letter that begins *Dear Sir/Madam or To Whom It May Concern*. Such salutations denote a lack of research and professional knowledge on the artist's part.

A cover letter should be short—two paragraphs maximum—and concise.

First Paragraph Use the first paragraph to introduce yourself. If you have a mutual colleague who's willing to let you use his or her name, this can be a great help. The colleague should be a collector, a critic, a curator, an artist the director knows and respects, or a very close friend of the person to whom you're writing. Don't use the name of a casual acquaintance of the exhibition director because an exhibition director is sure to have a thousand acquaintances and this won't help you get a meeting.

Second Paragraph Keep the second paragraph polite and simple. You may express, without demanding, your desire for a meeting or studio visit.

Do not delay sending a packet out because you fear writing the cover letter. Gallery and museum directors get a lot of artist's packets, and they aren't looking to be "wowed" by the letter. They are looking to be "wowed" by the artwork. Don't bog them down with lengthy ramblings. They want to get to the good stuff—your work.

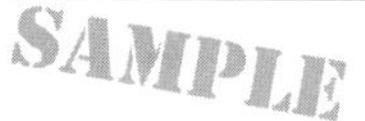

Dear Ms. Baxter,

My name is Jane Doe, and I am writing to introduce my artwork to you. A mutual friend, John Smith, recommended that I familiarize you with my work. I have enclosed a disk of 15 images, a résumé, and a statement.

I've seen several exhibits at your gallery this year, and I am impressed with the caliber of the artists that you show. I was crazy about the Joan Jones show in particular. I would like an opportunity to show you some of my work in person. I'll follow up in a few weeks to see if you have an interest in meeting with me.

Thank you for your time and consideration.

Sincerely,
Jane Doe

It's that simple!

Assignment: *Create a cover letter to a specific gallery.*

Exhibition Proposal

An exhibition proposal is different from a grant proposal. (See Chapter 10.) An exhibition proposal is usually listed in the submission guidelines of art institutions such as nonprofit art centers and museums. A proposal goes beyond the artist's statement because it conveys not only the deeper meaning of the artwork, but also why the work should be exhibited in this particular space. The way to convince your audience is to explain how your artwork fits into the mission of the institution and how you'll specifically utilize the exhibition space.

I have to confess that this is sometimes hard to do if your work doesn't fit into current trends in art, such as environmental awareness, or if your work is not site-specific, such as installation art. No doubt there will always be "hot" topics and media that are more in fashion than others. Institutions are naturally more inclined to jump on the bandwagon in order to demonstrate their contemporary relevance to their audience. You will have to make peace with this and be satisfied to do the work you do—or make some changes to address these issues in your artwork. Many artists who are hot today may quickly go out of fashion, and many artists who are committed to wherever their vision takes them wait a long time to achieve substantial recognition. There are no easy answers here.

I'm a painter, and I've seen a resurgence of painting in the art world in recent years. However, it can still be difficult to sell the idea of a painting show in many institutions. This is due to a current desire for interactive exhibits (exhibits that invite active audience participation) and those that educate children by addressing a variety of state standards in education. Often these demands are made on institutions in order for them to receive funding and to engage their communities. If you can show in your proposal how your artwork will meet the needs of the institution, you'll have developed a competitive strategy for securing an exhibition.

Assignment: *Create a proposal to an art institution in your community or in your region of the country.*

Chapter Notes

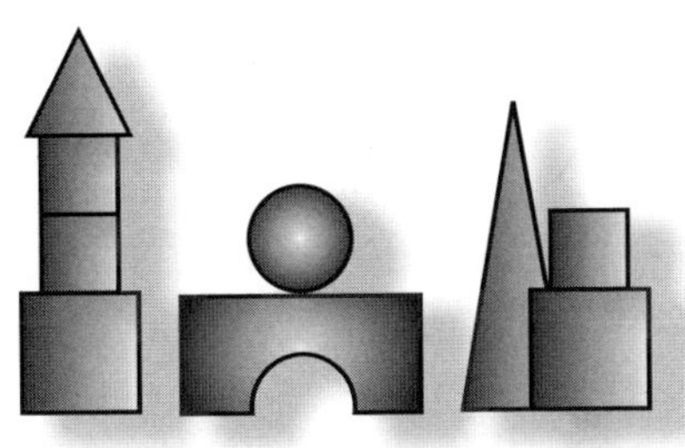

Chapter 10 *Grant Proposals*

As you progress along your career path as an artist, you are sure to hear about funding opportunities you would like to apply for. A grant proposal is a request for funding made to a government, public, or private organization. Typically, the grants available to artists are those that fund travel, education, or an art project one has already completed, is in the process of working on, or wants to initiate.

Most of the components that we discussed already—your visuals, résumé, and statement—are sure to be required in a grant application. However, there are other aspects to consider when applying for grants that I will cover here. While I'm not an expert in this field, I've written successful proposals that received funding both for my own work as an individual artist and for nonprofit institutions where I've worked. I've listed resources in the Appendix that give a more in-depth study of grant proposals, but in this chapter I'll emphasize some simple tips I know to be useful.

Is the Grant a Match?

The first thing to do when you receive grant application materials is to read carefully through the whole document. You can waste hours of time if you don't. You'll need to identify if you meet the eligibility requirements for the grant and to determine if your experience is commensurate with the opportunity.

Eligibility If you don't read the application thoroughly upfront, you may miss key requirements, such as geographical restrictions on where the artist must reside or the type of projects allowed. Some artists have difficulty reading and understanding guidelines. If you're easily overwhelmed by applications, I suggest asking a friend to help you.

Qualifications Once you've determined that you meet the eligibility requirements, you'll need to identify if you're a qualified candidate for a particular grant. Let me give you an example:

John Simon Guggenheim Memorial Foundation Fellowship

The average Guggenheim grant in 2008 was approximately $42,000. On the foundation's website grantees are defined as "advanced professionals." The site explains that an advanced professional is someone who has an extensive exhibition background. What they don't say is that most of the artists they have funded already had a national and/or international reputation. So to determine whether you're qualified, you must take your research a step further and look up (on the Internet) the artists who received grants in the past two or three years. You'll find that these artists not only have an extensive exhibition record, but that the exhibitions are often at the most prestigious art centers and museums, nationally and internationally. The Guggenheim folks aren't funding artists who have extensive exhibition records in Northwest Indiana.

In 2001 I looked into the Guggenheim Fellowship. Information at that time wasn't readily available on the Internet, but I wrote the foundation for guidelines. Here's what I discovered.

In that year, the Guggenheim Foundation gave out 183 awards to individuals in the arts and humanities.

There were 2,728 applicants; therefore, only six percent of the applicants received an award. Of the 183 grantees, only 33 of the awards went to artists (now we're down to one percent). The breakdown of artists by their disciplines was:

- 7 filmmakers
- 7 photographers
- 19 painters, sculptors, and installation or digital artists.

At that time, I determined I wasn't yet ready in my career trajectory to apply for a Guggenheim.

So remember to go over the guidelines thoroughly and always research past recipients of a grant. Look at the various recipients' personal websites. Read their résumés to see if your professional experience echoes theirs. You'll end up with a much better idea of whether you're a good candidate for a particular funding opportunity and save a lot of time and energy.

Application Process

When writing a proposal, address every item that the guidelines contain. If there's a checklist of items the foundation is interested in, reread your proposal several times and make sure you've thoroughly addressed every item on the checklist. For example, if a grantor's guidelines state that they fund projects that are of value to the community, then you must show clearly and concisely how your project will do that. You may need to present some evidence to convince the grantor that your work meets these guidelines. If the grant process involves answering questions on an application, be sure to mention how your project benefits the public, whether or not there is an actual question specific to this topic. If the priority is mentioned in the guidelines, the grantor expects the issue to be addressed.

Below I've taken the applications from one foundation and one residency and extracted a question from each to use as examples. Coupled with a sentence or two about the organization, I'll demonstrate the way I come to my own conclusions about which artists are well matched for these various opportunities.

Puffin Foundation

Puffin is interested in funding emerging artists, artists of diversity, and artists who haven't had much previous support. They're looking to support projects that are innovative and will advance progressive social change.

Briefly describe the project for which you are requesting a grant in 500 words or fewer. If you are collaborating with a community-based organization, educational or health institution, or another network in the distribution of your project, identify it. Attach a letter from the organization confirming their commitment to your project.

My conclusion

This grant is for a young, minority artist who creates work about social issues. Perhaps the project actually solicits participation from the community. Artists who already have a nonprofit institution committed to presenting their work will have an advantage. Puffin Foundation is looking for something specific and doesn't want an artist to stretch the concept too far. If you don't make work that is obviously about social issues, you'll be wasting the foundation's time and your own if you apply.

Jentel Residency: on a ranch in Wyoming at the foothills of the Big Horn Mountains

On a single separate sheet, describe the work you want to do at the Jentel Artist Residency Program. Address this question: Does your work explore or challenge the roots of generally held assumptions, values, and beliefs? If so, describe how and why.

My conclusion

This residency is for artists who will benefit from the location of the residency—the great outdoors—because they interpret the landscape or utilize it in some way in their artwork. In order to answer the question about whether the work challenges generally held assumptions, the artist will need to be experienced: either mid-career or an art school graduate. I think they're asking if the artist's work challenges social beliefs, but they may also be asking if the artist's work challenges assumptions about art or the artistic process.

Budgets

While residency applications do not generally require a budget, many grant applications, especially those for project grants, will ask you to submit one. A budget is a realistic account of how much money it will cost to carry out your plans as well as an accounting of income you expect to raise for the project. For instance, let's say your project is to produce a catalog of your work. You would like to print 100 copies and intend to sell each copy for $3. If you anticipate selling all 100 copies, one line of your income budget will show $300 for catalog sales.

Here are a few tips I can share with you if you are asked to submit a budget.

- Create a budget that is simple and clear.
- Donations, grants, and gifts received from other sources are looked upon favorably by grantors you are soliciting. Examples of this include a grant commitment from another organization, a restaurant donating all the opening-night refreshments, and a critic offering to write an essay about your work for free that will be featured in an exhibition catalog.
- Make sure the income and expenses are equal.
- Most grants ask you to explain the budget to some degree in your narrative. Make certain that you address

any complicated budget items.

There are a couple of terms you will need to know to create a budget that appeals to grantors.

- ***In-kind.*** An in-kind item is a service or a material that is donated to you (not a monetary gift). For example, if a graphic designer has agreed to create your exhibition postcard, then you can list the design fee as an in-kind item on your budget. You'll need to ask the designer what he or she normally charges so the value of the in-kind donation you list is realistic.
- ***Matching Funds.*** This means that the amount the artist is requesting from the grantor is being "matched" by another funding institution or by the artist's own money. Therefore, if the grantor requires matching funds, you need to show that the project costs twice the amount you're requesting.

If the funder requires a cash match, they are most likely not going to match the in-kind donations with cash. Therefore, the project needs to cost twice as much in cash expenditures as your request.

Sample Budgets

Example 1:

Your project is a solo show at a community art center. You have a letter of commitment from the art center. The exhibit will be presented one year from today. The art center usually charges a rental fee, but they've invited you to exhibit for free. The foundation you're applying to requires that you have a 50/50 cash match to your request.

Expenses	Cash	In-Kind
Art Supplies: (be specific and realistic)		
Paint	$ 100	
Canvas	130	
8 Stretchers (5' x 6' stretcher @ $60 each)	480	
Documentation (photographer and slides)	520	
1,000 4-color postcards	320	
Postage (400 cards)	88	
Space Rental		$ 300
Graphic Designer (postcard)		150
Total In Kind		**$ 450**
Total Cash Expenses	**$1,638**	

Income	
Artist's Funds	$ 819
Grant Request	819
Total Income	$1,638

Even though you're not allowed to use the in-kind amount toward the cash match, you want to list these amounts, as funders look favorably upon in-kind donations.

Example 2:

Your project is the same as above, except in this example the grantor doesn't require the 50/50 match to be a cash match. You could modify the budget as follows.

Expenses	Cash	In-Kind
Art Supplies: (be specific and realistic)		
Paint	$ 100	
Canvas	130	
8 Stretchers (5' x 6' stretcher @ $60 each)	480	
Documentation (photographer and slides)	520	
1,000 4-color postcards	320	
Postage (400 cards)	88	
Space Rental		$ 300
Graphic Designer (postcard)		150
Total In-Kind		**$ 450**
Total Cash Expenses	**$1,638**	
Total Expenses	**$2,088**	

Anticipated Income	
Artist's Funds	**$ 594**
In-Kind Donations	**450**
Income	**1,044**
Grant Request	**1,044**
Total Income	**$2,088**

Example 3:

You're applying for $1, 000 from a foundation. Your project is to produce a small educational and promotional brochure. You will print 1,000 brochures, most of which you will mail to curators, critics, and collectors. You anticipate selling 200 of the 1,000 catalogs for $1 each. You've also applied for a government grant for this project and anticipate receiving $600.

Expenses	Cash	In-Kind
Designer	$ 500	$1,000
Paper/Printing/Folding (1,000 brochures)	1,000	
Distribution (mailing supplies, postage)	400	
Forward written by critic	250	
In-Kind Total		**$1,000**
Total Cash Expenses	**$2,150**	

Anticipated Income	
Government grant	$ 600
Sale of brochures @ $1 each	200
Artist's funds	350
Income	**$1,150**
Grant Request	**1,000**
Total Income	**$2,150**

For further information on grants, please refer to the *Resources* section at the back of this book.

Assignment *Set a budget.*

Expenses	Cash	In-Kind

Anticipated Income	Cash	In-Kind

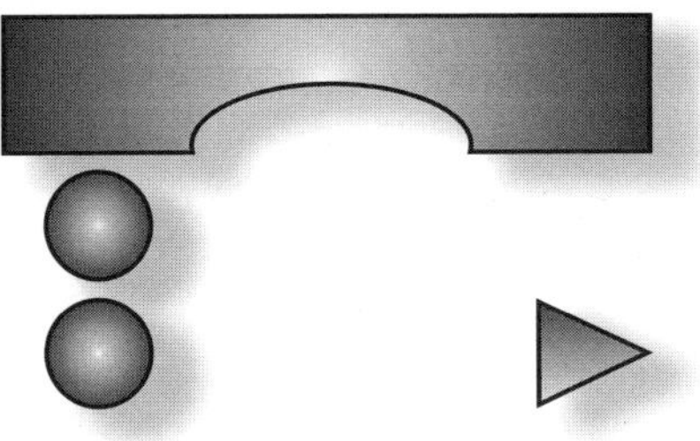

Chapter 11 *Websites*

Artists today often ask the question, do I need website? If you are wondering about this question, the answer is yes, you do. The Internet is an amazing resource that empowers artists to increase the visibility of their artwork and to promote it. However, it is better to wait and have a website planned than one that is poorly designed or doesn't function properly.

If you're just starting out in your art career, consider paying to have a personalized online gallery hosted by an art organization you respect. These collections of artists' galleries are also referred to as artists' registries. One major benefit to being part of a registry is that it costs less than creating and maintaining your own site. Also, you'll likely receive more visitors to your page than if you're out there on your own.

Another benefit is that patrons who are looking for a certain style or genre of art often visit larger sites that carry many artists, hoping to see lots of art quickly. Your work may be seen by someone who would never find your personal website. If you decide to go this route, make sure that the organization is respected and that the artists' galleries are well designed. Some examples of organizations that host online registries are Artists Space *(www.artistsspace.org)*, Woman Made Gallery *(www.womanmade.org)*, and the Chicago Artists Coalition *(www.chicagoartistscoalition.org)*.

There are hundreds of organizations operating these types of sites, so do your research to find the most suitable to your needs.

There are other options for websites and how to create one. Just as you visited galleries, visit websites of galleries and artists. Begin to think about what websites you like and how your work and ideas could best be presented on a website. You may also begin writing or collecting the content that is necessary for your website.

Determine whether you want to build a site using a do-it-yourself template or hire a designer to create your site. There are some do-it-yourself websites that offer an array of well-designed templates for a very reasonable fee. Artists can individualize the templates by choosing from a variety of fonts, layouts, and colors. However, you must have some technical computer skills in order to use these sites successfully, so if you are a technophobe, this path is not a good choice for you.

Template systems vary in functionality. For instance, some templates will allow images to be enlarged only to a predetermined size or will allow only a certain number of menus on your site. If you want the visitor to be able to enlarge your images to full-screen size or if you want more than five or six menu categories, certain templates may not work for you.

If you've decided to hire a designer to build your website, apply the same advice given earlier for finding a photographer. Insist on getting a list of websites that the designer has created. A reputable designer will be happy to provide this for you and probably has them listed on his or her own website. Go to and navigate through each of them to get a sense of the designer's abilities and aesthetics. Contact the artists and ask if they were satisfied working with the designer. Ask what their websites cost and if they would recommend the designer. There are those who will charge you plenty to create a website but do not have the needed computer skills or proper design skills.

Also be cautious of students or friends of friends who offer to build you a website for a few hundred dollars. The average starting cost for a professional website is $500, with the norm being more like $1,000 to $1,500. Do some investigating so you spend your money wisely.

Your next step is to revisit those websites you liked, especially those of other artists, and make a list of the ones you find most pleasing and easy to navigate. It's likely you won't like everything on one site, so make specific notes regarding what you like and what you don't like. Ask yourself what feeling you want to convey to people when they visit your site. Do you want it to feel more traditional or contemporary, minimal or explosive, formal or friendly? Talk over these points with your designer to make sure the two of you communicate well and that he or she understands your needs and wants for this website.

Register your own name or the name you will use as an artist with a domain name hosting company such as GoDaddy.com. Your name as an artist is important. Use your name consistently on all your information, whether it is your website, your résumé, or any other information piece. Do not sometimes hyphenate or use your married name or a middle initial. If your name is already taken for a website domain, try to find a solution that makes sense. For example, if *janetbloch.com* was taken, I would look for *janetblochartist.com*—rather than create a name such as *powerpainter.com*. That is too cutesy and would detract from my identity as an artist.

Create an outline of the information to put on your website. The different menu items you choose for your site can be created from your outline. For instance, one menu item should be your artist's statement. More than likely this menu item will contain only one page, but if you have created several bodies of work over your career, it is possible to put several statement pages that correspond to each body of work under the Statement menu.

The following are the most common menu headings that artists use on their websites:

Home Page

This is the first page a visitor sees.

If it's confusing or bland, they may not go further. A work of art placed here is very effective, as is an attractive layout with thumbnails of several artworks. Your name should be on the Home page too. You might have some brief text.

Gallery

This is where the visuals of your work should be placed. Your gallery may have several pages, each devoted to a different body of work or organized by the year the artwork was created.

Statement

Use your artist's statement or write something specifically for the website that describes your philosophy.

Biography

This is where a photograph of the artist goes, along with background information that is significant or interesting. It should be written in the third person and be a narrative of your professional achievements.

Résumé

Usually a résumé saved in a pdf file format is placed under this category.

Contact Information

In addition to information on how to contact you,

you include a field where visitors can leave their e-mail address and a message. This is a good way to build your mailing list.

Press

You might include links to articles related to your work or philosophy here—or include the articles in a pdf file format.

Store

Visitors can purchase artworks from you on this page. Your designer can set up a shopping cart feature for selling your work online. Convenient payment systems such as PayPal can be easily installed on your site and allow you and your patrons to conduct business safely.

Copyright notice

Usually appears as a footer on the home page and often is seen as a footer on every page. It can read "© year (or years), Artist Name. All right reserved."

Setting up your site:

Here are some helpful guidelines for setting up your website:

- You must have high-quality visual images of your artwork. No matter how well designed your website is, it will not make up for poor photographs, so get your photographs taken before you start putting up a website.
- Order your images on each page the same way as described for ordering images in your artist's packet. Let the images tell a story and flow.
- You need images of at least 10 works to make having a website worthwhile. It is preferable to have 20 to 50 images, depending on how long you've been working as an artist. More than 50 images is overkill even if you're famous.

- Do not use a logo unless you are in the field of commercial art or design.
- Do not use black or wild colors for the background of your website. White or a very pale gray are good choices because most artworks "pop" on these backgrounds. There are exceptions to all rules, but if you want to be the exception, you must break the rule brilliantly.
- Put a photograph of a compelling piece of your artwork on the Home page. A photograph of you is optional, but if you use one, put it on the Bio page.
- Steer clear of too many bells and whistles. While music, animation, and lots of graphics might be perfect for some websites, they are generally not great additions to an artist's website. The art should be the ingredient people want to keep coming back to the site to see.
- Keep websites simple, clean, and clear of clutter. Keep the text short and concise. Articles you or others have written about your work can be saved to separate pages.

Assignment: ***Step 1.*** *Visit several websites and make a list of layouts and functions you like and dislike.*

Step 2. *Begin an outline of the content for your website. Decide what headings you will need and how many bodies of work you want to display.*

Chapter Notes

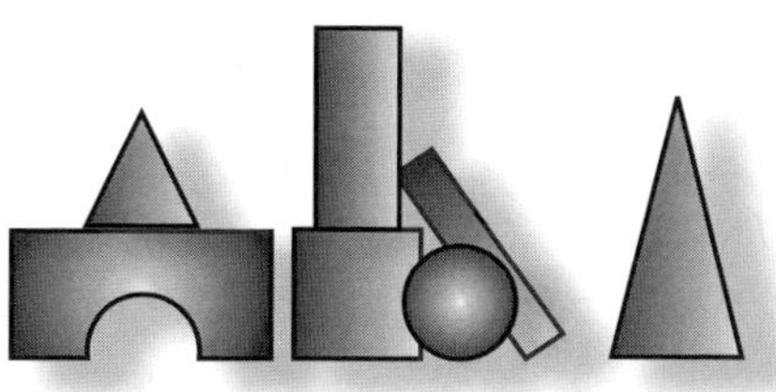

Chapter 12 *Strategic Planning*

I've given you a lot of information to digest. You may be feeling overwhelmed and a bit beleaguered about how to get where you want to go. I've found that the most effective antidote to this feeling is to create a *strategic plan.* Another term for a strategic plan is an *action plan,* and action is the key to success.

Again, I want to emphasize that action is desirable. but rushing isn't. I once read that the famous painter Ivan Albright spent five hours painting each square inch of canvas. While I'm not asking you to slow down to that extreme, it must be noted that Albright created numerous masterworks in his career. He knew what needed to be done to achieve what he wanted. So keep in mind that steady, unfaltering action will get you to your goal.

In my work with clients, I've found that breaking down a strategic plan into six-month increments produces optimal results. Six months has proven to be a long enough time to make real headway and a short enough time to stay focused on the goal.

Here's how to proceed

Look back over your answers to the questions in the Starting Point section in Chapter 1. Over the course of working in this book, your answers to these questions may have changed. Add any further information about your progress to your earlier answers. With these notations in mind, make a list of three goals you believe to be realistic and achievable in the next six months.

Now review these goals and scrutinize each of them to see if they are steps on the path to the Big Vision that you described in Chapter 1. Let's take one example and go through the process together.

Example 1 My Big Vision is to be sought after for public art commissions.

Starting Point Answers

1. I haven't yet completed a body of work that lends itself to this goal.
2. I've exhibited in many national group shows that had jurors of critical stature.
3. I've had many solo shows in galleries.
4. I know what my work is about, but I'm not clear how it will fit into a public art venue.

Six-Month Goals: Version 1

1. Make a study of successful public art projects.
2. Create new artworks that lend themselves to being exhibited as public art.
3. Send out three packets for more solo shows.

Sample Analysis: Goal 1 relates directly to my Big Vision.

Without studying public art I won't understand what types of works and projects are currently being commissioned. It is vital to my big vision to be familiar with the various materials and trends being utilized in contemporary public art projects.

Goal 2 also relates directly to my vision.

I need to develop a body of work in order to submit competitive proposals. My research shows me that I need 10 to 20 images of work that are connected in order to submit a packet. Knowing my pace and available time, I determine that I can realistically create three new pieces in six months.

While Goal 3 has merit . . .

I've already had enough solo shows to establish my credentials in this way. Another solo exhibition at this time shouldn't be a priority. Submitting packets for exhibitions takes time and energy, and if I'm successful in securing another solo show, putting it together will take even more time and energy. If I'm serious about my Big Vision, I can no longer spend time on projects that deplete my energy, as I won't have enough vigor to achieve my heart's true desire. I'd be better off developing my statement for public art projects by journaling and completing the exercises in this book.

Six-Month Goals: Revised Version

1. Make a study of successful public art projects.

2. Create new artworks that lend themselves to being exhibited as public art.

3. Create a core statement that can be customized for public art submissions.

Assignment: *Taking this same example, look again at your three top goals. What actions can you take each month to achieve these goals? Write down as many things as you can think of.*

Examples

- Journal about the meaning of my artwork.
- Answer the questions in this book about my new artwork.
- Go to public art websites and spend one hour a week looking up projects and reading about them.
- Buy a book about public art or subscribe to a public art magazine.
- Invite a friend to lunch who I know has done a few public art projects and ask if I may conduct an informational interview.
- Set aside 15 hours every week to sculpt.

To create the plan, first determine the actions that are a priority. You can't seriously pursue a public art career if you have no artwork that relates to the public domain. Therefore, spending 15 hours a week sculpting is a priority. Look for the actions that need to be done continually and consistently and write down those actions in every month for the six-month period.

Now turn your attention to the actions that are one-time activities. Where in your six-month plan could those one-time activities be most effective? Perhaps you determined that taking your friend to lunch to ask her questions should happen after you learn more about public art. You decide to do some reading first so you don't waste her time and yours getting information that's readily available elsewhere. It would be best to get your friend's more nuanced information after you've done your research, so you decide to ask her to lunch in the fourth month of the action plan.

One of the most challenging yet beneficial characteristics of a six-month strategic plan is that it forces you to eliminate all activities that won't bring you closer to your six-month goals. It helps you see that actions such as "Make crafts for holiday gifts" or "Attend a conference on art licensing" just don't fit in your plan right now. It doesn't mean you won't ever do those other things; it just means that for the next six months you'll make the concerted effort to take only those actions that serve your vision.

You begin to see why reaching your goal has proved difficult in the past!

Assignment: Create a Six-Month Strategic Plan.

Six-Month Goals

Write down three big goals you would like to accomplish in the next six months.

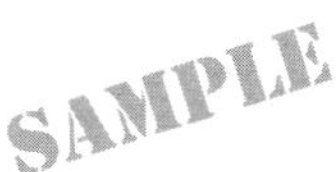

Goal 1. Make a study of successful public art projects.

Goal 2. Create new artworks that lend themselves to the genre of public art.

Goal 3. Create a statement for public art submissions.

1. ____

2. ____

3. ____

SAMPLE **Month**	**Strategic Action Steps** Write down three actions you can take each month to bring you closer to achieving one or all of your goals.
May	1. Create in the studio 15 hours every week.
	2. Go to public art websites and spend one hour a week looking up projects and reading about them.
	3. Answer the statement questions in Chapter 7 of this book about my new artwork.
June	1. Create in the studio 15 hours every week.
	2. Go to public art websites and spend one hour a week looking up projects and reading about them.
	3. Journal about the meaning of my work.
July	1. Create in the studio 15 hours every week.
	2. Go to public art websites and spend one hour a week looking up projects and reading about them.
	3. Journal about the meaning of my work.
August	1. Create in the studio 15 hours every week.
	2. Invite a friend to lunch who I know has done a few public art projects and ask if I may conduct an informational interview.
	3. Journal about the meaning of my work.
September	1. Create in the studio 15 hours every week.
	2. Buy a book about public art or subscribe to a public art magazine.
	3. Journal about the meaning of my work.
October	1. Create in the studio 15 hours every week.
	2. Read the public art book or magazine for an hour a week.
	3. Answer the questions in this book about my new artwork again.

Six-Month Goals:

Write down three big goals you would like to accomplish in the next six months.

1. ______________________________

____

____

____

____

2. ______________________________

____

____

____

____

3. ______________________________

____

____

____

____

Month	Strategic Action Steps Write down three actions you can take each month to bring you closer to achieving one or all of your goals.
	1.
	2.
	3.
	1.
	2.
	3.
	1.
	2.
	3.
	1.
	2.
	3.
	1.
	2.
	3.
	1.
	2.
	3.

Month	Strategic Action Steps Write down three actions you can take each month to bring you closer to achieving one or all of your goals.
	1.
	2.
	3.
	1.
	2.
	3.
	1.
	2.
	3.
	1.
	2.
	3.
	1.
	2.
	3.
	1.
	2.
	3.

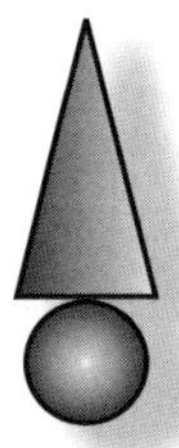

Chapter 13 *Travel Highlights*

The journey you are on is certain to have its ups and downs. As you put your art out in public more frequently, rejection will be a normal part of the process. Your disappointment will vanish when you begin to experience successes as well. If you follow the advice in this workbook, you'll begin to receive exhibition acceptance notices and follow-up phone calls or e-mails from galleries that you've submitted your packet to. If they are interested in showing your work, you'll be faced with a whole different set of challenges.

What to Bring

One of the most exciting moments for an artist is when a gallery follows up after receiving your artist packet. Often the gallery director will ask you to come in for a meeting and bring some work so the staff can view it in person. They always want to see the actual work before making a decision. The first time this happened to me, I went into a tailspin. I had no idea what to take or how to prepare.

Look over the images of work in the packet you sent out. Remember, you were supposed to keep a record of this information. They like what you sent them, so bring in some of the actual work depicted in your images—or something very similar. Don't bring work that is going in a new direction. If you're going in a new direction, you need to be thoughtful about whether or not the new work is still a good fit for the place where you sent the original packet. It will present a dilemma if it is not in keeping with your previous work.

If the size and weight of your art is manageable, bring four or five artworks with you to the gallery. Wrap the work in large pieces of bubble wrap with little tape. You don't want to spend a long time unpacking and packing your work. The first time I did this, I was in a nervous sweat, with pieces of bubble wrap everywhere!

If your artworks are too large or heavy to take to the gallery easily, invite the director to your studio for a visit. An artist's studio may vary from a shared loft space outside the home to an artist's dining room. Regardless of the space, it's not advisable for others to be present at your studio during the visit. If you have studio mates, I would ask them ahead of time to leave the studio for an hour. It is nerve-wracking enough to be in a vulnerable situation without other people sitting in on it. Take some deep breaths and try to organize your work in the studio so it is accessible and easy to view.

Bring Yourself

Well before the studio visit, think about why you chose to send your work to this particular venue in the first place. If you have made a sincere study of the venue and other artists who have exhibited there, the conversation should flow smoothly. Avoid talking too much and never gossip. Let your visitor observe your work and ask you questions about it.

Remember to breathe and be yourself. Refrain from being pushy. There's no merit in talking someone into showing your work who isn't truly supportive. This book is taking you through a process; having faith in that process can make a positive difference. You're on the road to success. There's no one circumstance that can make or break your career. Many opportunities will come to you as a result of your dedication to your art. Be true to yourself, and the situations that are right for you will unfold. Don't hang all your hopes and expectations on one person, gallery, exhibition, or grant. It takes only one person who champions you to give you a chance.

These positive messages have helped me conquer adverse or fearful conditions. I'm confident that I act with integrity and that the outcome of a situation is never a mistake. When things don't go the way I'd like, of course I feel disappointed. But the faith I have in my journey, and in myself and my artwork, has made the difference between feeling like I'm a success or a failure, between moving forward or giving up.

Pricing

Only discuss price if your visitor is interested in your work and expresses a desire to show it. Galleries almost always take 50% of the retail price of the artwork. Your previous research should have revealed what the price for work that is similar to yours is at this gallery. Therefore, if a photograph by one of the gallery artists goes for $2,000 and it is the same size and presentation quality as yours, you can use this as a base. If the photographer has a greater reputation than yours, then the price of your photographs may have to be lowered.

If the gallery director asks you how much your work costs and you respond that you want $5,000 for your piece, the next question is likely to be, "How many works have you sold for $5,000?" It will sound foolish if you reveal that you've sold work for a maximum of $500 up to this point. The director will wonder how you arrived at the $5,000 figure. On the other hand, you'll sound knowledgeable if you tell him or her honestly that you've sold many works for $500 and are hoping to raise the prices somewhat by working with the gallery. Telling the director you're willing to work together to settle on a figure that the market will bear shows good business sense.

What to Wear

Dress comfortably. This is not the same as a job interview, and nobody expects you to wear a suit. However, I wouldn't wear paint-soaked or clay-covered clothes either. Wear clean clothes that allow you to move effortlessly. Feeling comfortable has a positive effect on one's mood.

Following Up

At the close of your studio visit, you will probably have a good sense of whether there is further interest in your work. Either way, send a handwritten note thanking the person for his or her time and attention. If the interaction leads to the promise of a future opportunity, follow up the note with an e-mail in a couple of days. Reiterate your understanding of the discussion. When in doubt, ask questions and clarify points to avoid confusion later.

If you can't meet with a gallery owner in person, most of these issues can be resolved via e-mail and phone calls. In place of a studio visit, you may be asked to send several pieces of your work so the gallery personnel can review it in person. In this case, you'll need to negotiate who pays the shipping costs. It's usually split equally by the artist and the gallery.

Framing

If your work needs to be framed, make sure the frame you pick is fairly simple in its style. Ornate frames or frames that are embellished with fabric are not good choices because they look old-fashioned and fussy. If you want to be an exception to this rule, you must prove to be impeccable in your taste and make a convincing connection between your work and the framing. Stay away from spring-loaded metal frames as well, for while they are low-priced, they also look it. Better choices are stained or painted wood frames with simple lines and a bit of depth to give the artwork more substance.

Plexiglas® (acrylic plastic in sheet form) is now the standard covering for drawings and prints as opposed to glass, which is very heavy and can shatter. If a mat is needed (most prints and drawings should be matted), the mat board should be a neutral color: white, off-white, or black. Colored mats look busy, even garish, and draw one's eye away from the artwork rather than enhance it. Mats should be cut with beveled edges. Unevenly cut mats look unprofessional, so if you are not able to cut a perfect mat, go to a reputable frame shop to have it done.

All framed works should be securely wired on the back for hanging. Saw-toothed hangers are not reliable devices to ensure hanging stability. If an artwork is too large or heavy for wiring, D-rings placed on the back are effective. Make sure the rings are at the same height on the left and right sides of the work so the piece will hang level.

If the work is three-dimensional, it should sit on a floor or pedestal (or hang from a ceiling) with stability. If an artwork can be easily tipped over, it's very likely to do so at an art opening. It's the responsibility of the artist to design works and presentation devices with this in mind. The gallery staff's responsibility is to present your art properly and safely, but it is not their responsibility to steady an unsteady work of art.

Packing and Shipping

If the exhibition is out of town, you'll need to pack and ship your art. If you're sending three-dimensional work, follow the advice of Beate Minkovski, Executive Director of Woman Made Gallery. She teaches interns to pack fragile pieces as if they are packing their grandmother's china. If you can jostle the piece around in the box, it will likely break. Cushion artworks sufficiently. Anyone who has ever unpacked a lot of artwork will beg you NOT to use packing peanuts. There are many places that actually forbid their use because they are a huge nuisance, clinging to everything and impossible to get off the floor.

Two-dimensional work can be packed by putting a piece of cardboard over the Plexiglas® and then wrapping the whole work in bubble wrap. Use brown packing tape to secure the bubble wrap so it's visible when cutting open the bubble wrap. Then pack in a sturdy, reusable carton so that the art is secure and doesn't move when handled. Make sure the boxes are all secured well and labeled properly.

There are many shipping companies to choose from, and I suggest calling around and getting quotes from several before deciding on one. Find out each shipper's policy regarding artwork and their insurance limits. I've found both UPS and FedEx to be suitable to my needs, but if you create large-scale sculptures or unusually shaped fragile pieces, you might have to use a company that specializes in shipping art. The responsibility for paying shipping costs to and from a group show falls on the artist. For solo shows, institutions' policies vary. Some places split the cost with the artist. Larger, more venerable institutions often cover shipping for a solo exhibition, but an artist shouldn't assume this; instead, get all policies and agreements in writing up front.

Be grateful for all opportunities.

If certain ones don't go exactly as you hoped, think of them as great practice for your future successes.

Chapter Notes

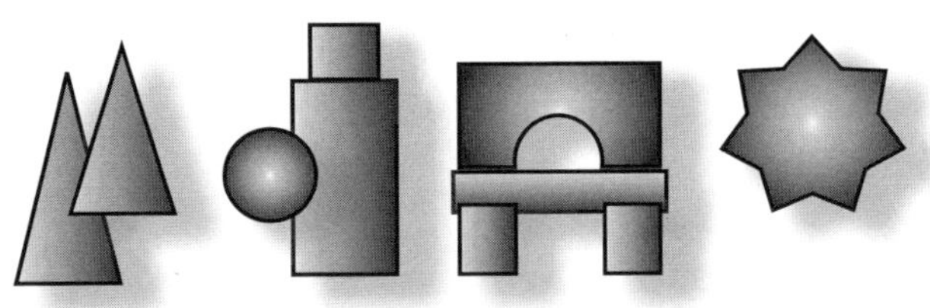

Chapter 14 *You've Got a Solo Show!*

After all of your hard work and focus, you will delight in seeing your dreams come to fruition. Imagine that you've just been offered your own solo exhibition. There are two main scenarios in which this might take place. One is in a commercial gallery, and one is at a nonprofit institution. Let's examine both situations so you'll know how to proceed.

The Gallery Experience

Both commercial galleries and nonprofit institutions schedule their exhibitions at least a year in advance. Sometimes galleries have a slot they didn't fill or a show that was cancelled. If you're offered that slot, make sure that you can be ready with a body of work before you agree to it. All artists I know push themselves when they are having a show, but you need to be realistic and leave yourself a reasonable amount of time to create your pieces.

I've been represented by three different commercial galleries in Chicago. In all three cases, I've signed a consignment agreement when I left work in the gallery. The agreement describes the work by title, medium, size, date it was completed, the retail price agreed upon, and the percentage the gallery takes. Most often the percentage that commercial galleries take is 50 percent of the retail price. The agreements I signed also allowed the gallery to negotiate discounts for their customers, up to 20 percent, that would be split 50/50 by the artist and the gallery. For example, if a work retailed for $3,000, I agreed to let the gallery negotiate the selling price down to $2,400. The $600 discount would be absorbed by each party at $300 each, so I would receive $1,200 for the work.

I've never had a contract that asked me to keep my work exclusive to a gallery. I caution artists against this unless the gallery is extremely well known for selling out shows and catapulting the careers of their artists. The only U.S. cities in which this would be likely to happen are New York and Los Angeles, so for most artists signing an exclusivity contract is not desirable. However, there are certain rules of ethics I advise you to follow whether you have a contract or not.

Reputable commercial (for-profit) galleries are happy for the artists they represent to show work in nonprofit museums and art centers, because those institutions can enhance an artist's reputation. If you're included or awarded your own show at a nonprofit venue while you're represented by a commercial gallery, you'll have to work out the details of any sales agreements with all parties. Often the commercial space and the nonprofit agree to split 50 percent equally, still leaving the artist a full 50 percent of the sale price.

However, no commercial gallery wants you to have a show down the street or a few miles away in a competing commercial gallery. They also don't want you to sell your work from your studio for a lower price than they are selling it. If you do this, you are undercutting your gallery—and yourself in the long run. Why in the world would a gallery want to work with you if you do this?

Many artists envision the gallery/artist relationship as adversarial. Instead, the relationship is a mutual business relationship. It works well when both parties come to an agreement that suits each of them. If you aren't happy with the terms offered to you, don't agree to them. You may want to consult a lawyer before signing, particularly if it's your first showing or contract. The information the lawyer gives you about contracts will aid you in understanding future contracts and what the negotiating points may be. You can also check with other artists the gallery shows and ask them if they're happy showing with the gallery and if they feel the gallerist is reputable. Again, there's research to be done. I've found when artists aren't happy with their gallery, they'll tell you—if they trust that you'll be discreet.

Here is a breakdown of responsibilities as they are shared by the artist and the commercial gallery in most instances. These must be confirmed verbally and in writing in each case.

Responsibilities of a Commercial Gallery

- Designs and pays for printing of postcard announcement
- Gives the artist at least 100 announcements to use at his or her own discretion
- Pays for mailing announcements to the gallery's list of patrons
- Pays for opening-night expenses (usually wine, water, and light snacks)
- Installs the work
- Generates all gallery signage, title cards, and price lists
- Insures the work while on the premises
- Writes and sends press releases to media, including critics, newspapers, and websites
- Provides appropriate staff during regular gallery hours
- Handles sales of the artwork
- Provides record keeping and collection and reporting of state sales tax
- Makes payment to artist for sales no later than 30 days after the show ends

Responsibilities of the Artist

- Delivery of the artwork on time and at artist's expense
- Pays for mailing announcements to artist's patron list
- Sometimes helps install work
- Behaves professionally and adheres to gallery policies
- Records and reports income for individual state and federal income taxes
- Picks up work when agreed upon

The Nonprofit Institution Experience

Nonprofits vary greatly in their reputations, sizes, and budgets. Smaller institutions can provide a wonderful means to expose an artist's work to the local public. The nation's leading cultural institutions can greatly advance an artist's career or signify the highest achievements of an artist. Because of the vast differences in each institution's budget and resources, the responsibilities they can take on may differ greatly. These should be understood by artists who have done their research.

Division of Responsibilities in a Nonprofit Institution

Every bullet point in the lists of responsibilities for the Commercial Gallery and the Artist is up for negotiation when you're dealing with a nonprofit institution. If the institution is large, such as a museum, an artist can expect its responsibilities to be similar to that of a commercial gallery. If the nonprofit is small and low on resources, an artist needs to be realistic about what is reasonable to expect. Small nonprofits struggle to make ends meet and often exist to give emerging artists an opportunity to show their art they may not otherwise have.

If you're expected by a nonprofit to install and host your own show, here are some items you will need to be mindful of:

Signage

Each work of art needs its own title card. The easiest way to do this is to format a business card on your computer. Sheets of perforated business cards that can be used with most printers are available at office supply stores. You can get business-card software or make do with a word-processing or page-layout program. Each card should have the title of a work, along with its medium, size, and price. Some venues discourage artists from putting the price of the work on the title card; in that case, you will need to make a price list. You want your patrons to be able to identify the works on the price list easily, so make sure all the titles are consistent on your cards and on the list.

If you have enough money in your budget, there are companies that produce vinyl lettering that looks extremely professional. This lettering is often used for artist's names and show titles at larger institutions. The lettering can be produced at any size, in a variety of colors and styles, and is burnished right onto the wall. If this is not affordable, simply printing your name and the title of your show on a piece of 11" x 17" paper and mounting it on a white board is fine.

Installation

Here is a list of items that will be useful when installing your own exhibit:

- ☐ Hammer
- ☐ Nails or screws of different sizes
- ☐ Large and small levels
- ☐ Yardstick or tape measure
- ☐ Removable mounting squares, which work well for hanging exhibition signage and title cards
- ☐ Adhesive wall putty, which is also useful for signage or keeping a painting straight
- ☐ Pencil and sharpener

- ☐ Address/comment book, which can be used to build your mailing list
- ☐ Pens
- ☐ A good friend to help you, as it's difficult to hang a show without an extra pair of hands and eyes

Wherever your exhibit takes place and whoever actually installs the art, I advise you to place the work carefully. It is difficult for the eye to take in artworks that are crowded together. Each piece needs room to breathe. Every space is different, so there are no rules to follow, but try to restrain yourself from using every piece to fill up space. Bring more work than you will actually need and be ruthless in your assessment of what makes the best exhibition.

Vanity Galleries

Artists should beware of another type of gallery, known as a vanity gallery. A vanity gallery is a space whose owners make all of their income from renting the space to artists, but deceives artists by pretending to be prestigious. Vanity galleries have terrible reputations in the art world—and rightly so. Their personnel have no artistic credentials, they do not try to market or sell artists' work, and they feed on an artist's insecurity and desire to feel accepted. Artists are first enticed by a notification that they have been "selected" by the gallery for a show. After they are hooked, they are told there will be a fee. I've been solicited by galleries proposing to show my work for anywhere from $1,000 to $5,000. This differs from small amounts of rent that an artist may be asked to pay to have a show in a reputable nonprofit.

One way an artist can differentiate between a vanity gallery and a reputable nonprofit is to ask the institution if it has a 501(c)3 status. This means that the institution has received tax-exempt status from the federal government. In order to receive this status, they had to submit rigorous narratives, bylaws, board information, and financial audits. You might also search the Internet for the credentials of the people who run the gallery. Another way to differentiate between the two is to talk to other artists or contact state or county art advocacy groups. If you're asked to pay more than $600 in exchange for any solo show, I advise you to walk away.

Exhibition Announcements

If you are expected to design your own postcard, get started two months before your show. The first thing you need to do is choose a piece of your work for the announcement. The artwork you select should be eye-catching and representative of your exhibition. Postcards are not a great place for subtleties, and the purpose of the announcement is to get people to the exhibit. Stick to one image for a postcard. More than one image crowds an already small space. In addition, the photograph of the work on the card must be of excellent quality.

There are websites for designing postcards that are easy to use and reasonably priced. My personal favorite is Vista Print *(www.vistaprint.com)*. Have a friend who is attentive to details proof the copy before you place your order. The most experienced professionals will confirm how often they make mistakes when they proof their own designs.

Organize your personal mailing list a month before the show. Try to get your postcards in the mail at least two weeks prior to the opening reception. Do not buy mailing lists of galleries and critics from marketing companies. This is a waste of money. If you really want a particular gallery director to see your show, your odds will be much greater if you write a personal note to the director.

Your audience will begin with your family and friends. Do not pooh-pooh this idea. They are your staunchest supporters, and when you're starting out, these are the people most likely to purchase your work and come to your exhibitions. Treat them as the valuable assets that they are.

Opening Night Enjoy yourself. Openings receptions are meant for artists to celebrate the fruits of their labor. Get there early and stay late. Mix and mingle. Buy yourself a new outfit. If it suits your style, feel free to dress eccentrically. You really can't overdress for an opening. The way you present yourself can make an impact on future patrons of your work. In other words, looking great can boost your sales. This is your red-carpet event, so look as handsome or as gorgeous or as artsy as you can.

Tonight you are the star!

Chapter Notes

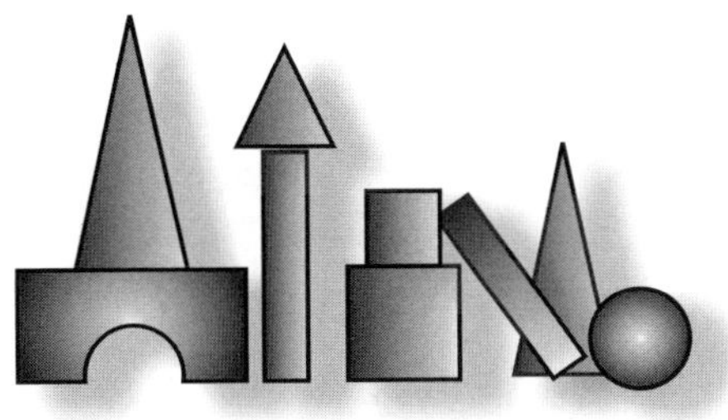

Chapter 15 *The End of Our Tour*

I hope you found this workbook to be useful in building your career as an artist. I know that there are topics I could have written more about, but my goal was to produce a book that is user-friendly and not overwhelming. If you've done the assignments in this workbook, I'm certain you've taken many steps forward in your art career. This isn't the end of your road, of course, but it does conclude our time together—for now.

Years ago, my sister and I were taking a quiz about finding your passion, and I told her, "I just love to make things." For whatever reason, artists don't seem to have a choice about being an artist. It's a bit of a cliché, but it's true: we create because we must. It isn't rational, for there is work that is certainly less demanding, more lucrative, and easier on the ego. But artists need to be artists, and I'm happy to be one of them. Artists are creative thinkers, productive citizens, and some of the world's great problem solvers—and the world needs more of us. If I've encouraged you on this road and have given you advice that helped you advance your dream or gain some recognition for your work, I'm more than satisfied.

I'd love to hear from you about your experiences with this workbook. Some of you will have worked through this book alone, some with a friend, and some in a classroom. It will be useful to me to hear all of your critiques so that I can continue to devise helpful workshops and materials for artists. You may contact me at *janetbloch@frontier.com.*

Good luck to you, and as my friend, artist Ethel Peterson, says: ***"Productivity always!"***

Chapter Notes

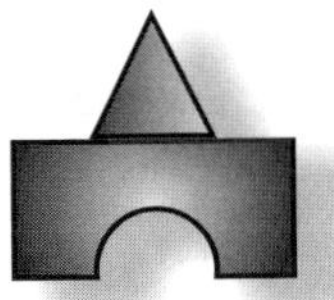

Acknowledgments

Writing this workbook was a longtime goal of mine. I love to teach and facilitate workshops because I like to interact with people and talk. For me, writing is much more difficult and requires more discipline. My satisfaction at writing down this information for artists is immeasurable. I couldn't have done it without the following people:

- My husband, Bobby Talamine, and my sister, Rosanne Poppell, who lift me up and love me whether I'm up or down (and believe me, I've been both). Bobby has taught me about passion and determination, and Rosanne is my teacher, best friend, and soul mate. I don't take their support and the closeness we share for granted.
- Beate Minkovski, my dear friend and colleague, who is the Executive Director of Woman Made Gallery in Chicago. Without Beate and her courage, hard work, passion, and love for artists, I wouldn't be able to contribute the information in this book. Together, we developed the original workshops on which this workbook is based—and shared the desire to help artists through education and encouragement.
- Joan Chesterton and Pamela DeNeuve, for their love and support, both practical and spiritual. They are both great teachers and mentors.

- Melanie Deal, a wonderful artist and the editor who helped me shape this material. Her expertise and suggestions were spot-on, and her encouragement inspired me to keep writing and clarifying information.
- Jennifer McCord, a talented consultant and coach. If I hadn't met her, I would never have finished this workbook. I consider our meeting one of those meant-to-be life changers.
- Beatrice Fisher and her family, Deena Linett, Lisa Merida-Paytes, Corinne Peterson and Aimeé Picard for the permission to use images of their artwork in this workbook.

Finally, this book is dedicated to all the workshop attendees and dear clients, who over the years have allowed me to comb through their materials. They have trusted me to give them constructive criticism and steer them towards their strengths. They have let me pick apart their statements and résumés, and assess their artwork (sometimes brutally). I dedicate this book to them, and I consider it a privilege to have been let into their lives and their art.

—Janet Bloch, January 2011

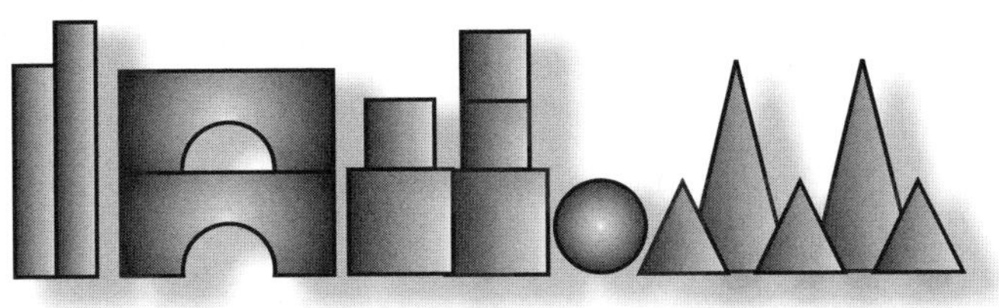

Resources for Artists

This list of resources is by no means comprehensive. It is, at the time of this writing, a list of my favorite known resources. I don't mean to exclude the many fine companies and professionals who are surely out there. Please ask artists in your area for their recommendations as well.

Picture Framing Supplies

- **Light Impressions**
  PO Box 940
  Rochester, NY 14603-0940
  800-*828-6216*
  www.lightimpressionsdirect.com
- **American Frame Corp**
  Arrowhead Park
  400 Tomahawk Drive
  Maumee, OH 43537-1695
  800-537-0944, *www.americanframe.com*
- **Metropolitan Picture Framing**
  6959 Washington Ave South
  Edina, MN 55439-1506
  800-626-3139
  www.metroframe.com (website has framing tips)

Packing and Shipping Supplies

- **Pro-Pak Professional Packers, Inc.**
  527 Dundee Road, Northbrook, IL 60062-2801
  847-272-0408, *www.propakinc.com*
- **Airfloat Systems, Inc.**
  PO Box 229, Tupelo, MS 38802-0229
  800-445-2580, *www.airfloatsys.com*
- **U-Line**
  1-800-295-5510, *www.uline.com*
- **WoodenCrates.org**
  www.woodencrates.org/findacompany.html

  or find a crating company near you!

Photographers in Chicago

- **Cindy Trim**
  Oak Park, IL
  Home:708-383-4207
  Cell: 312-806-3221
- **Tom Van Eynde**
  Chicago, IL
  708-214-7416

Digitals Only

Make digital image into slides through the Internet

I Print From Home, *www.iprintfromhome.com*

Resources that list Grant and Exhibition Opportunities for Artists

- **CAR** (free)
  Chicago Artists Resource
  www.chicagoartistsresource.org
- **Chicago Artists Coalition** (Must be a member)
  www.caconline.org
- **The New York Foundation for the Arts - NYFA** (free)
  www.nyfa.org
- **Artist Trust (free)**
  www.artisttrust.org
- **Art Deadline.com**
  www.ArtDeadline.com
  Income & Exhibition Opportunities for Artists
  Full Internet Version $24 annually
- **Art and Healing Network** (free)
  www.artheals.org

Recommended Publications

Helps to find exhibition venues around the country

- **Art in America**
  Annual Guide to Museums, Galleries and Artists
  Comes out in July/August
  Available in bookstores or by subscription
  1-800-925-8059
- **New American Paintings**
  www.newamericanpaintings.com

Web Designers

- **Camille Winer Art & Design**
  312-203-7301, *Camille@camillewiner.com*
  Designer for artists' websites
- **Keyword Design LLC**
  219-923-5279, *judith@keyworddesign.com*
  Designer for artists' websites
- **Other Peoples Pixels**
  www.otherpeoplespixels.com
  Do-it-yourself websites
- **Heavy Bubble**
  www.heavybubble.com
  Do-it-yourself websites

Recommended Printer

- **Vista Print**
  www.vistaprint.com
  Economical, good quality, easy to use for business cards, invitations, posters, etc.

Recommended Publications

For more information on grants and public art proposals

- ***The Artist's Guide to Grant Writing: How to Find Funds and Write Foolproof Proposals for the Visual, Literary, and Performing Artist***
  by Gigi Rosenberg
  Random House, 2010
- ***The Artist's Guide to Public Art: How to Find and Win Commissions***
  by Lynn Basa
  Allsworth Press, 2008